AC WHAT YOU WANT IN LIFE:

MANAGE YOUR MIND FOR SUCCESS

By Michael Dillon F.S.S.M. Ph.D. (Hon)

Published by New Generation Publishing in 2014

Copyright © Michael Dillon 2014

First Edition

The author asserts the moral right under the Copyright, Designs and Patents Act 1988 to be identified as the author of this work.

All Rights reserved. No part of this publication may be reproduced, stored in a retrieval system or transmitted, in any form or by any means without the prior consent of the author, nor be otherwise circulated in any form of binding or cover other than that which it is published and without a similar condition being imposed on the subsequent purchaser.

www.newgeneration-publishing.com

New Generation Publishing

CONTENTS

Acknowledgements 7
Foreword 8
Review 10
The Negative Pyramid Of Life 13
Prologue 15
The Fisherman 19
Notepad 20
Chapter One: The Subconscious Mind 22
   The Subconscious; A Powerful Support for
   Change 22
   Subconscious Mind Exercises 23
   The Garden of Your Mind 25
Chapter Two: Actively Using Subconscious Mind
Exercises 29
Chapter Three: Relaxation 31
   What Is Relaxation? 31
   The Tension Trap 31
   Stress Control - The Role of Relaxation 32
   How Do We Change? 32
   Changing Your Mind Patterns 34
Chapter Four: The Process Of Relaxation 37
   Breathing 37
   The Count 38
   Creating Your Special Place 39
The Whale 42
Chapter Five: The Mental Laws Of Success 44
   The Mental Law of Self-Awareness 44
   The Mental Law of Cause and Effect. 46
   The Mental Law of Belief 47
   The Mental Law of Control 49
   The Mental Law of Attraction 51

The Mental Law of Expectation 53
Chapter Six: Self-Awareness 55
  Do You Value Your Life? 56
  Asking The Right Questions 57
  Positive thinking 63
  Working Positively With Your Subconscious Mind 65
  The Subconscious Mind Exercise 67
  Looking Towards a Positive Future 68
  Your Journey of Discovery 70
Chapter Seven: Negative Inner Dialogue 72
  Asking the Right Questions 77
  Parent Relationships 79
  Dealing With Feelings 80
  Exercises for overcoming negative mind chatter: 83
  Subconscious Mind Exercise 85
  Cabinets & Dustbins. 86
Chapter Eight: Self-Belief 89
  Forgiveness 89
  The Self-Belief of Infancy 93
  The Power of Unconditional Love 94
  Handling Negativity with Humour 97
  A Clearer Path Ahead 98
  Using Experiences Positively 99
  Living In the Present – Not The Past 99
  The Observing Self – Using the Past Positively 100
  Subconscious Mind Exercise (One) 103
  Subconscious Mind Exercise (Two) 104
  Chain, Rope String and an Elephant 105
Chapter Nine: Sharing In The Abundance Of Life 108

    Asking the Right Questions 108
    The Choice is Always Yours 109
    Believing In You.. 113
    Handling Fear.. 114
    Working Effectively With Your Subconscious Mind. 116
    Subconscious Mind Exercise 117
    The Sunflower... 118
Chapter Ten: The Confidence To Be You 121
    The Mirror of Self... 123
    Subconscious Mind Exercise 129
    Mind Software... 130
    The Subconscious Mind Exercise 134
    Perceptions Of Belief.................................... 135
Chapter Eleven: Creating The Future You Desire. 137
    Asking the Right Questions 138
    Time is of the Essence 140
    A Brighter Future.. 141
    Your Book of Life... 146
    Subconscious Mind Exercise 148
    Searching For Shangri-La 149
Chapter Twelve: Using The Mental Laws Of Success Positively... 152
    Working Effectively With the Subconscious Mind. 152
    Subconscious Mind Exercise 153
Chapter Thirteen: Detachment............................ 155
    Working Effectively with your Subconscious Mind. 162
    Subconscious Mind Exercise 165
    Using Positive Self Talk 166

How You Can Gain The Maximum Benefit From This Book 168
    Focused Learning 170
    Write Down Your Ideas 170
    Turn Diary Notes into Positive Action 170
    Notepad Questionnaire 172
Conclusion 175
About The Author 177
Glossary 180
Last Words 184

ACKNOWLEDGEMENTS

I have studied the work of many motivational psychologists and professionals in the 'talking therapies' who have influenced me during my years as a professional therapist.

I would like to mention the following for their particular influence in some of the content contained in this book.

Brain Tracy, Dr Wayne Dyer PHD, Hans Christian King, Robin Skynner, Dr Robert Maurer, Jack Black and Deepak Chopra

I am indebted to my good friend Chris Smith for his suggestions and advice with the organising, presentation and editing of the material in this book.

I am very grateful to my daughters Susan and Patricia who I am so proud of. They have always been an inspiration for me, also my grandchildren Alex, Rosanna, Zach and Ella for the joy of just being with you. Thank you also Alex for your computer skills in helping me with certain aspects of formatting the book.

A very sincere thank you to all my clients who have come to me for help over the last twenty years, without the experience of working with you this book would never have been written.

I can't leave out Charlie (the family dog) for his forbearance in often having to wait for his daily walk while I was busily working on the book.

Finally and above all, my wife Peggy for the unconditional love she has shown to me through all the many years we have been together and the moral support she gave me when I gave up a successful commercial career to become a therapist. Her patience and understanding through the many hours I spent in my office creating this book was just one example of her kind and generous nature.

FOREWORD

It is an intrinsic human quality to look for ways in which to protect or improve our sense of well-being. Sometimes this is aspirational; built upon a confident expectation that we deserve and can achieve better, or perhaps the tentative hope is to redeem a lost happiness in the face of overwhelming anxiety or depression. Either way, a perfectly rational aim is energised or distorted by powerful emotional 'drivers'. There is a way to manage these 'drivers' but using emotional intelligence to create a bridge to self-development is often a major challenge for many people. They often believe they have the skills and ability to change their lives in a positive way but are held back, experiencing difficulties with low self-belief, negative emotions and disappointing behaviours. These can be daunting to overcome. However, the author goes to some lengths to explain, in a psychological context, how the brain works and how this knowledge can be used to improve the quality of a person's life in many positive ways.

This book takes you on an interesting and informative adventure in closing the gap between emotional intelligence and self-development. It can open the creative mind to new possibilities for positive change. The book is an interwoven journey of discovery in many intricate ways that are nevertheless simply interpreted. You, the reader, are invited to embark on a personal journey, using the subconscious mind in an effective and positive way. The only limits are set by your readiness to think, observe and explore.

In forty years working as an educationalist and more latterly in mental health I know that people are capable of attaining even more than they might have dreamt. Often the missing key is that of wise counsel and guidance. This book provides that missing key. It is not the 'quick fix' that needs the buzz of a motivational 'high' – the words are easy but it's no good leaping up to the heavens if you can't fly. This book invites you to make *yourself* a bit of a priority in your life and take time to read and mull. The writer gently draws in the reader to consider such low-key but mind-blowing effective concepts as 'detachment' and 'abundance' and shows you how to work with them. This is not a place for jargon or mystique; it is plain language for you or me, the person in the street. This book is about giving you options and finding your own way. That way you can trust the progress you are making and feel emboldened to take the next step... and the next. This book is the key – your dreams are your own.

Chris Smith

Chris Smith has an education degree from Oxford University and an advanced diploma in education from London. He has taught in Zambia and the UK, later with advisory, training and project management roles in curriculum development at secondary and tertiary levels.

From 1993, when he attained a diploma in hypnotherapy and stress management, to 2010, Chris ran a successful hypnotherapy practice and was a Founding Fellow of the Society of Stress Managers. He has worked with clients with severe and enduring mental illness for the charity **Mind**, *which was in partnership with a local NHS mental health trust. Latterly as deputy manager of Day Services there, he developed a new model of support for individuals with mental health difficulties. The* **Momentum** *programme enabled service users to move their own lives forward and monitored outcomes over time. Chris is Director of Training for WellMind Ltd.*

REVIEW

The mood and style of this book is positive throughout. The book does not indulge the reader with reasons why you cannot achieve what you want in life. Instead, it suggests you become aware of what is stopping you, and asks the important question 'If I had what I wanted in life, what kind of person would I be?' This dispenses with spending large amounts of time analysing problems and enables you to use your time in finding out what you **need** to do to achieve your goals and realise your ambitions, dreams and aspirations.

A special feature of the book is the number of metaphors that complement the various chapters in the book and provide insights into the psyche, and the kind of traps that keep people locked into habitual behaviour that has long since lost its purpose.

The metaphor that especially resonated with me is the story of the elephant staked to the ground as a baby. Unable to escape from its tether, the baby feels helpless. Every day just the strap around his legs is sufficient to remind the young elephant of its limitations. Even when fully grown, the elephant does not seek to escape its tether. This metaphor is appropriately used to illustrate the obstacles we believe are real, which prevent us reacting positively to our challenges in life.

The timeless chapter on detachment explains how you can avoid stress, anxiety and fear when you want to achieve something. It creates the space and freedom to achieve what you want in life, instead of having to crunch again and again through a thousand affirmations. The book explores that quiet place deep inside that can get you off the starting block and move your life, **positively**, in the direction that you want.

The book provides a great way for those who are perhaps on their initial steps, to realising what they need to do to become happy and successful or whatever they want to achieve in life. However even I, as a seasoned practitioner of self-development, gained new insights and awareness that I was delighted to receive. I certainly gained some information that I hadn't expected to discover.

The author has worked hard to produce a format in his book that makes the exercises **accessible** and **achievable**.

Jenny Lynn (BA) has a joint Honours Degree – Modern Language Studies (German/Spanish) and has studied at Seville University and the Paedagogische Hochschule, Hildesheim. (BA). In 2000 she undertook a 3-year course to retrain as an intergrative Psychotherapist, Counselor and Hypnotherapist and has subsequently developed an integrative approach for the treatment of Chronic Fatigue Syndrome.

Jenny's professional memberships are a Fellow of The National Council of Psychotherapists, and a member of the Hypnotherapy Association, General Hypnotherapy Register and as an individual Member of the British Association of Counselling and Psychotherapy.

She has supervised, trained, mentored and coached her colleagues to work transpersonally and holistically during her time as a practicing therapist.

During 2013 Jenny and a colleague launched the Open Mind College, which is specifically for the development of the therapist's personal integrity, congruency and professionalism, so they can lead the therapy world into a more enlightened age.

Jenny is a prolific writer, blogger and newsletter writer engaged in sharing information on personal development. She has ebooks available online

"Unlocking the Mysteries of Chronic Fatigue Syndrome – Therapist Training Manual" and a number of self-help downloadable ebooks.

TheOpenMindTherapist.com

THE NEGATIVE PYRAMID OF LIFE

We feel out of harmony with ourselves to the degree we feel we are controlled by circumstances, undesirable emotions and behaviour, resulting in:

FEAR

ANXIETY

NEGATIVE EMOTIONS

LACK OF CONFIDENCE

LOW LEVELS OF SELF- ESTEEM

LOSS OF CONTROL, REDUCING OUR QUALITY OF LIFE

THE POSITIVE PYRAMID OF LIFE

We feel good about ourselves to the degree we are able to:

- CONTROL FEAR
- COPE WITH ANXIETY AND STRESS
- ESTABLISH POSITIVE FEELINGS
- ENJOY GENUINE SELF-CONFIDENCE
- HAVE GENUINE FEELINGS OF SELF-ESTEEM
- CREATE A GOOD QUALITY OF LIFE

PROLOGUE

As I progressed through many years experience as a professional therapist, it became clear to me one of the most important skills required in achieving a life of success and happiness is emotional and behavioural competence. This concept is therefore dealt with in this book as a vital part of a person's self-development.

My purpose in writing the book is to provide a 'reader participation' experience. It is designed in such a way that the reader can actively engage his or her mind positively during the various exercises that are shown at the end of each main chapter of the book.

It is my experience that many people who are keen on self-development read many books, most of which they find interesting and stimulating. So they try and change, but frequently nothing happens, at least not permanently. The most frequent reason for this is emotional turbulence. People don't have much of an idea as to how they can use all the interesting and stimulating material they have read in their everyday lives, in an effective way. As you go through this book you will discover profound but simple ways to change your life. The book covers the important bridge between self-improvement and emotional competence.

With my work as a professional therapist I have encountered persuasive, anecdotal evidence that those people who enjoy the greatest happiness, both in their family and social lives and in the workplace, have significant skills in emotional and behavioural competence, both in respect of their own behaviour and dealing with others in a caring and positive way.

It seems clear to me that people with the ability to communicate effectively and deal with their own and other people's negative emotions and behaviour, have the most important skill, that set them apart from others. These are the aspects of human behaviour that many people in the past have considered a sign of weakness to even think about, never mind acknowledge. Focus on, or learn about. Emotions and behaviour sensitively handled can help motivate and encourage people to achieve the happiest outcome in any situation, including parenting skills.

Emotional awareness enables a person to stay calm, cool and collected when facing obstacles and challenges, and helps an individual to work at high levels of performance in all areas of his/her life. Most people are now adequately educated and this will increase as the 21st century progresses. Those that are not so numerous, some may say even rare, are people in control of their emotions and behaviour. These people have a significant advantage over others in all areas of life and find that people are more likely to respond positively and co-operatively because of the personal skills they possess. This is in marked contrast to the outdated way of thinking that views feelings, emotions and behaviour are just something that get in the way, and are to be discarded as being of no great importance.

The new world dominated by electronics has and will continue to change our lives in many remarkable ways. We are more than ever before confronted with the most important challenge of all:

How can we achieve a life of success, happiness and fulfilment?

The fragmented societies of the 21st century in the western world provide very little help for people with their emotional and behavioural self-development. They tend to establish division rather than unity, separation rather than togetherness and relentless competition rather than co-operation and support. The focus is upon separated individuals, rather than a single united group or community. Emotionally our society just throws people in at the deep end, to either sink or swim. We don't get much help or support towards getting to know ourselves, or to find that deep sense of inner peace, enjoyment, meaning or purpose in life.

This book is essentially about the basic mental resources needed as a foundation on which the reader can build a successful, happy and fulfilled life. If the book is approached with this in mind the reader can become intimately involved with the suggestions, ideas and subconscious mind exercises the book contains. You can then realise how it could help you to become the person you really want to be.

> **Being the person you really want to be. How about that for an achievable goal?**

Think how it will be, by reading this twenty-first century book, you are able to cope with all that society throws at you, in a calm, relaxed and effortless way, helping and encouraging you to cope effectively and be an achiever in the twenty-first century.

This book engages your conscious mind in the suggestions and ideas included in the main text. Your subconscious mind connects with the 'subconscious mind exercise' and various metaphors at the end of each chapter. Therefore the reader is engaged in balanced mind learning, using your whole mind and not just part of it.

As you go through the book it will help you, in an unobtrusive way, to move towards personal happiness in your own way, and that is always the best way for you. All you have to do is believe you can achieve what you want to ... and you can.

You may feel this book doesn't have anything to do with you and I wouldn't tell you it does. That is a decision you can make for yourself. However if not now, it's possible it may be relevant to you sometime. So if you believe prevention is better than a cure, reading this book is valuable for you too. At any time in the future, you will know what you need to know, at the time you need it.

Think of how good you will feel when you realise you are being supported in many positive ways to obtain effective skills that can positively help you to become the person you really want to be.

> **We do not need to keep shovelling out the darkness. All that is necessary is to turn on the light.**

So let us go forward together as two friends on an exciting journey of discovery, heading towards the goal of a wonderful healthy, happy, successful and fulfilling life for you

The Fisherman

A villager pleading hunger approached a fisherman and asked if he could have some fish from that day's catch. The fisherman politely refused the request.

Later the same villager returned and again asked for some fish, just not understanding why the fisherman would not give him some. Again he met with a refusal. The villager just could not understand why the fisherman would not give him a few fish to survive each day on.

The villager returned again, hungry and astonished by the fisherman's meanness. Finally he asked what he had to do to get some fish.

Simple replied the fisherman.

"Give me your time and I will teach you the art of fishing!"

Tell me and I'll forget

Show me and I may remember

Involve me and I'll understand

NOTEPAD

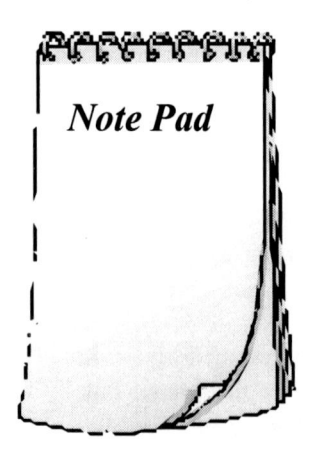

A notepad has been included in this book to help you look into specific ideas that you would like to examine in more depth.

It provides added value to the book, as writing ideas and thoughts down instead of trying to keep them in your memory is a very supportive thing to do. It can help to clarify your ideas in a clear way and enable you to examine particular aspects of the book which you feel will be especially helpful for you.

You can support what you learn from reading this book and carry out the subconscious mind exercises by jotting down your ideas - by using the questionnaire at the end of the book. Making written notes of your ideas is a very useful support to the reading process. As you come across an idea or exercise that particularly appeals to you, write it down and think about it. Examine its potential value to you and how it could help you change and improve.

Until thoughts and ideas are linked with action, little or nothing is accomplished. The notepad is designed to help you with this activity. Decide what you need to do and how you can apply it in your life and then write a short action plan and take appropriate action.

I suggest as you go through the questions for each applicable chapter, and have examined the question in more detail, tick the relevant question box. This will help you keep a record of these important questions.

Use a diary or lined notebook of some kind so you can write down your ideas as a written record of those parts of the book which you feel will benefit you most by a closer examination.

Using a written notepad to jot down your ideas will help you to take control of these ideas and take immediate action in your daily life.

A notepad logo, as above, is placed randomly at the bottom of some pages in the book to remind the reader of the notebook section.

CHAPTER ONE: THE SUBCONSCIOUS MIND

Every reader of this book has the power to build and create the life they desire. By using the power of your own mind, you can create powerful imagery, frequently called visualisation, together with positive thoughts and feelings and do so with persistence and purpose as an active process for change. If you mirror within yourself that which you truly want to influence your life, you can do away with false limitations you have placed upon your positive development in the past, leaving those limitations in the past where they belong. Imagine how you will feel, when you are certain that you have changed all the things you wanted to change about you and your life, with belief and conviction, instead of continuing with all that old past uncertainty and lack of belief in yourself- so you can now say, "I can do it."

> **Change should into could, and try into I will do it!**

The Subconscious; A Powerful Support for Change

To change your behaviour you must change the way you think. Being unable to make use of your subconscious mind constructively and positively can stand in the way of becoming the person you want to be. Because your habits are controlled by your subconscious mind, your conscious choice to change negative habits presents a difficult challenge. You can resolve to change those aspects of yourself that you see as an obstacle in achieving your full potential, but then your subconscious thinking directs you to repeat your past behaviour and way of thinking, reinforcing past experiences of failure.

The very act of attempting consciously to solve what is fundamentally a subconscious mind problem can actually make the matter worse. There can be hardly anybody who has not experienced wanting to change in some way or other and not being successful in doing so.

Why is your subconscious mind so resistant to change? There are clear indications that behaviour and ways of thinking, learned and reinforced over long periods of time, become part of your emotional make-up, which is the element in your subconscious thinking that is most resistant to conscious attempts to change.

The normal way you are aware of your subconscious thinking is in dream states, either daydreams or at night. Your subconscious mind is also active when you visualise, that is create pictures on the screen of your mind with your eyes closed. It is at work, too, when you engage in habitual behaviour (often with that perpetual internal voice or inner dialogue as it is called).

The activity of your subconscious mind is much faster than your conscious mind. It does its own thing, completely outside your conscious control, without you having made any real conscious choice. However, its job is to protect you, to keep you safe and secure, it wants to be on your side, but at the same time is impervious to adult reasoning and logic. If you don't tell it what you want it to do, it will never know.

Subconscious Mind Exercises

The subconscious mind exercises in this book help you to re-programme and change your subconscious mind thinking in a way it can understand. When you do that it can be a powerful ally in helping you to achieve a successful and happy life.

Your subconscious mind is always on the alert and waiting to know how you want to be as a person. How you want to feel, behave and what you desire to achieve. Unless you regularly make it clear how you want it to help you and in a way it can understand, it will just do its best in a haphazard way. As soon as you open up a positive connection with the subconscious then you can move towards directing what it does and how it can assist you. The only other thing needed is persistence of purpose. It needs to be programmed and shown time and time again how you want it to fulfil your desires.

> **Gary Player, the famous South African golfer, one of the most successful golfers of all time, when told by a journalist he was a lucky golfer, replied. "It's funny you know, the more I practice the luckier I become."**

Your subconscious mind can assist you in making many personal breakthroughs and gain insights that could never be achieved with conscious thinking alone. It can give you constant, caring support and unfailing wise advice when you know how to make contact with it in a direct and positive way.

You could spend your entire life without even knowing what you can achieve by unleashing the full potential of your subconscious capabilities. After many years as a practising professional stress manager I have witnessed people make very positive changes in their lives. However those people came to me for help with specific problems. This book works in a generic way so the basic mental resources needed for a happy and successful life are dealt with.

The Garden of Your Mind

It has been known, for a long time, different sections of the human brain are responsible for specific functions. Research has shown that both sides of the brain engage in decidedly different ways.

Each hemisphere of your brain has its own information-processing system that works in its own way. While they often act in tandem, each can act independently of the other. The left hemisphere, the conscious mind, uses logic to solve problems; it is analytical and judgemental. Your subconscious mind (the right hemisphere) relies on emotional, intuitive experience and right brain assertion. Behaviour you developed in childhood, over long periods of time, can be impervious to your adult reasoning and logic. Your subconscious mind is the storehouse of your long held attitudes towards behaviour and it does not distinguish between desirable and undesirable attitudes.

This difference can cause you serious conflict, and when the conclusions of the two sides of your brain conflict with each other, one side (usually the subconscious mind) will eventually dominate the other. A common example is the overweight individual or the smoker who consciously want to lose weight or stop smoking, but find they sabotage all efforts to do so. The left brain's conscious script may say, "I'm going on a diet" or "I'm quitting smoking", while the subconscious decides, "it's not going to happen, I need to do what I always do to cope with life."

No matter how committed you consciously are to improve your behaviour, your subconscious mind, because of a deep inner conflict, may allow you to go against your common sense, against your own best interest. As long as these conscious and subconscious scripts remain in conflict, there is no prospect for success. The challenge is to get the messages for change into both parts of your mind.

During the subconscious mind exercises in this book, your brain is offered a new behavioural script to follow. This overrides previous negative thought patterns, habits and undesirable behaviour, supplementing them with positive, assertive and achievement-orientated ones. Both parts of your brain are engaged with the process, therefore there isn't the usual conflict involved when you try to change using only your conscious mind thinking.

> **Alter your expectations from negative to positive. Positive and assertive expectations change your beliefs. When you start believing you can – YOU CAN**

You can make changes by conscious mind will power alone, however this rarely works when you try to change your feelings, emotions and behaviour. When both sides of your brain are working in unison, then re-programming your debilitating negative thought patterns is much easier.

The subconscious mind exercises in this book, when used persistently, can be effective for you in achieving lasting change because the source of your difficulties, the negative conditioning you have picked up during your life, is in your subconscious mind and it is in this part of your mind that changes need to be made.

Negative patterns of behaviour can be reprogrammed and changed in positive ways. Your subconscious has learned behaviours over the course of a lifetime, especially in childhood. Those behaviours recur as the brain sends a conditioned response based on times, places, moods or emotions. However you can be assured that because all behaviours are learned, they can also be unlearned. They can be replaced by encouraging the subconscious mind to react in more appropriate ways. During the subconscious mind exercises you can guide yourself into a state of relaxation, being aware of what is going on around you, but deeply rested and calm. In this natural state you can access your subconscious mind to promote positive changes for your own well-being.

You create your tomorrows by what you hold in your mind today. The same as you have created your today by what you have held in your mind in the past.

In the garden of your mind, if you allow your mind to dwell on failure, lack of success, lack of confidence, lack of self-esteem and allow stress to take over, weeds will grow naturally. Weeds do not need any fertilizer or special nurturing they just grow.

Subconscious mind exercises help you to take control of your subconscious thought patterns. You can dwell on positive, assertive and successful thoughts. You can boost your confidence and self-esteem whenever you need to, by holding in your mind powerful visualisations of yourself, as successful. You can imagine being the person you want to be with the characteristics you desire, uprooting the weeds and replacing them with beautiful flowers. You may not be a gardener, but you certainly know what weeds can do to a garden and how differently it looks when filled with colourful flowers.

However, don't feel you should somehow try to force change to happen. Just cultivate an attitude of relaxed attention. Let nature take its course, because attention and intention make any desired changes grow stronger and stronger in your life. Positive changes soon become apparent if you consistently use your mind as suggested in this book. First there is a sense that worries are disappearing. Then you don't feel overwhelmed by life. Things may go wrong, but they don't bother you as they used to. In fact the more they used to worry you the less they do worry you.

> **Many aspects of your character you would like to change are actually learned behaviours and responses, nothing more than that.**

CHAPTER TWO: ACTIVELY USING SUBCONSCIOUS MIND EXERCISES

The subconscious mind exercises included in this book require a quiet, relaxed state of mind to be effective as you work with your emotional mind. This is where your beliefs, habits and behaviour are established. It is this part of your mind that you get in touch with, whereby deeply ingrained negative beliefs, habits, behaviour or patterns of thinking can be changed.

To gain benefit from the subconscious mind exercises it is favourable to focus your awareness inwards. To help you in achieving this inward focus each exercise starts with a relaxation process with your eyes closed, so you can easily change your awareness from external to internal.

When your focus of awareness is inwards (something like day dreaming), you will discover you are able to deal with negative emotions and make behavioural changes in a much more relaxed way. Your subconscious mind is a storehouse of memories, knowledge and possibilities, so the more you can contact this storehouse of knowledge in an easy and effective way, the greater benefit you obtain. This helps you to use your inner resources positively, as you learn easily and naturally to change invalid beliefs and behaviour thoroughly and effectively.

> **You have all the resources within you to achieve any changes about your personal self you desire to change.**

Repetition is how the subconscious mind effectively learns and changes, not by big extravagant gestures, but by quiet contemplation, step by step, but in significant ways. So repeating the subconscious mind exercises, as often as possible, is vital in achieving the changes you desire.

Because the subconscious mind exercises encourage a conditioned response:
➢ The more you engage in them and the techniques you learn, the more you gain from them.
➢ The better you get at using your mind in this new positive way, the more useful it becomes to you.
➢ The more useful it becomes, the more you want to do it.
➢ The better you get at it, the quicker you get into a positive feedback cycle.

Everybody deserves some time during each day for himself or herself. You do. You've earned it. You've earned that time. So take that time for your own benefit and enjoy it. Yes make that commitment to yourself right now, to engage in the exercises every day. After all you're using your own natural resources, learning more about them, how to use those resources to bring you reward and satisfaction, all through your life.

The more you relax, the easier it is to use the positive mind patterns in beneficial ways and the quicker it helps you bring into your reality any changes you desire to make.

CHAPTER THREE: RELAXATION

Regular relaxation does far more than merely reduce stress. It positively helps to move you in the direction of your goals.

What Is Relaxation?

Relaxation is more than the absence of tension; it is the positive feeling of well-being you get that comes from just "letting go." It is freedom from the conditioned habitual tension that can cause you to perform at a fraction of your potential for much of the time. This is not to suggest that tension, in itself, is wrong. It is wrong only when it makes what you are trying to do more difficult.

The Tension Trap

Like most people you have a lot to do, with often little time to do it. This can mean that over the years you condition a state of tension so deeply into your nervous system and can respond to even the most minor of situations in a do-or-die way. There is then the danger of becoming ensnared in the "Tension Trap." You become tense and stay tense without ever realising why. Soon even the slightest inconveniences get blown up into major setbacks and if you are not careful you may start to make up reasons why you cannot succeed instead of acting upon the truth that you can. By developing a relaxation habit you begin to free yourself from this highly destructive tension pattern and feel much more relaxed and comfortable.

Stress Control - The Role of Relaxation

The foundation of stress control and release of unwanted feelings, emotions, and behavioural patterns is relaxation. Most people have a natural ability to quickly achieve a state of relaxation. In this relaxed state you are able to close down your awareness of what is going on around you, and pay greater attention to your own internal needs.

By repetitive use of the deeper relaxed state, you can focus on resources hidden from your conscious awareness and discover skills and abilities that you have, which are quite separate from your conscious mind skills. This is a different part of your mind, which can be used for personal benefit. You then develop a more positive way of thinking and consider your true feelings in a relaxed and controlled way, by releasing unwanted thoughts and feelings and encouraging character-friendly ones to replace them.

How Do We Change?

When you want to change emotions and behaviour, like most people, you try to do it by only using conscious mind thinking. As an infant, when you learnt the complex skills of sitting up, standing, crawling, walking, running and talking, you did not constantly judge and analyse what you were doing you just did it.

Who do you think learns more quickly and thoroughly: the adult, trying to cope with stress, anxiety and emotional challenges
   or
   the child learning the much more difficult task of how to sit up crawl, walk, talk and run?

The child every time, because children don't sit in judgement on themselves, they just take action and do things in natural and creative ways.

The most effective way to deal with negative feelings, stress, anxiety and undesirable behaviour is consciously to analyse what you are doing that isn't helping you to become the person you want to be, and then using your subconscious mind to correct the unwanted behaviour. When you try and change, using will power alone, it uses up your energy at an enormous rate and causes tension, anxiety and other negative thinking that rarely helps in bringing about the positive change you desire.

The alpha relaxed state of mind is a supportive conscious state in which to make emotional and behavioural change. The subconscious mind exercises included in this book enable you to work effectively with your subconscious mind. You can encourage this relaxed state of mind by closing your eyes, deepening your breathing and going down within yourself focusing on internal feelings and imagery.

There are two main motivations for change: curiosity and frustration. Curious as to how you can change and frustrated with how you are thinking, feeling and behaving in the present. Without these two motivations present you will find it difficult to change. Curiosity is clearly the essence of chapter 6 on self-awareness. Curious about whom you really are. So you are not just drifting along believing you are the person other people say you are, or believing your own superficial, negative beliefs about yourself.

Changing Your Mind Patterns

Your brain produces patterns, neurological pathways inside your nervous system, by bio-chemical changes. These are the result of your perceptions of experiences and events that have happened since the day you were born. Once these patterns are formed, they are difficult to change, because in the mind you follow them subconsciously and automatically.

When you start controlling your inner dialogue and internal imagery you start changing your mind patterns in a positive way, much more in line with the person you want to be. You stop allowing your thought patterns to be formed by chance and therefore take control of the 'steering wheel' of your life.

If you are not in a relaxed state when you are trying to change emotions and behaviour, it is like trying to select a single lottery ball, when they are all spinning around frantically, it's just pure chance.

If you relax and stop all the frantic spinning about and let the lottery balls rest peacefully you can select whichever ball you want and in the order you want them.

So when your mind is quiet, at peace and focused, you can take hold of the 'steering wheel' for change and not leave it just to chance. Whenever possible the ideal situation for working with this book is to relax your mind and body. Try this…

> 1. Take several deep breaths in and out, saying silently in your mind:
>   *"I relax deep inside."*
> 2. Raise your shoulders, get them as close to your ears as you can, hold the tension, then as you breathe all the air out let your shoulders drift down and allow the relaxation to travel down through your body to your fingers and toes. [Do this several times until you feel comfortable and relaxed.]
> 3. Focus on your breathing and drift down within yourself by creating peaceful and pleasant internal imagery, for instance, imagine yourself somewhere out in nature. It takes a relatively short time to do and the more you practise it, the less time you need to do it.

This will give you a few minutes to just settle down, relax your mind and body, clear your head of everyday concerns and gain the maximum benefit from reading this book. When your focus of awareness is inwards (something like day dreaming), you can discover you're able to deal with negative emotions and make behavioural changes that are much more difficult, if not impossible to do in a state of worry and anxiety

Your subconscious mind is a storehouse of memories, learning and possibilities, so working effectively with it you can really begin to understand yourself in a much more profound way. If you take the time, you can learn in a complete and thorough way. The more you leave the everyday world behind and are just in the moment, the greater benefit you'll obtain. As you learn easily and naturally, to use your inner resources positively, you can change invalid limiting beliefs and behaviour, thoroughly and effectively. Isn't it good to know you have all the resources within you to achieve any changes about yourself you desire to change? All you need to know is how to utilize the resources.

The more you relax, the easier it is to use the subconscious mind patterns in this book and the quicker it helps you bring into your reality the changes you want to make. Like most people you rarely have time to do everything you want to do each day, but there is time to do those things that are most important to you. So reading this book until you understand the contents thoroughly and completely, persistently going through the subconscious mind exercises, is a clear indication of how important you feel the changes you want to make in your life are.

CHAPTER FOUR: THE PROCESS OF RELAXATION

Read the following texts on this and the following page and become familiar with them. They describe a way of relaxing easily and completely.

Before you start this relaxation process be somewhere that is comfortable and safe, when you don't need to be alert to anything around you. You can close your eyes at any stage during the relaxation process. (It is normally easier to relax with your eyes closed.)

Breathing

Isn't it comforting to know you can relieve stress, anxiety and tension by just focusing on your breathing? So first of all focus on each breath, as you breathe in and out. Then deepen your breathing and make the breath out longer than the breath in. Take several deeper breaths in and out and as you let each breath out, say to yourself silently in your mind.

"I relax deep inside."

Do not strain to go too deep at first. As you practise this relaxation you will find a depth that is just right for you. By the time you have taken several deeper breaths, in and out, you will have already realised how true it is that tension can be relieved relatively easily.

The Count

Count down slowly from ten to one breathing deeply. As you release each breath imagine yourself drifting down deep inside.

With your eyes closed imagine you are looking at each part of your body as you count down from 10-1 and as you relax each part of your body you focus on.

10. Toes and feet

9. Ankles.

8. Calf muscles.

7. Knees.

6. Thigh muscles.

5. Waist.

4. Stomach.

3. Next raise your shoulders and get them as near to your ears as you can, hold the tension for a few moments then relax your shoulders all the way down until they are settled and comfortable. Now allow this comfort to travel down your arms to your hands right down to the tips of your fingers… then down your body to your feet and toes.

2. Then relax your head, forehead, eyes, ears, mouth and neck right down to your shoulders.

1. Take a final deep breath in and out and relax your spine and chest

Creating Your Special Place

As you quieten yourself with your eyes closed, you can go to a place deep inside where you just exist. A place away from the endless chatter that is going on in your mind, where there is a different kind of consciousness.

This is where positive change can most easily take place. You can create this special place in your mind, deep down inside you. Many people, when creating a special place, prefer it to be somewhere out in nature, by the seashore or in the hills or mountains, perhaps by a bubbling stream or a peaceful lake, or maybe in a wood or forest. It can be inside or outside, or an entirely magical place created entirely by you.

It is your choice. Wherever you decide your special place is, make it a place where you feel safe and secure, peaceful, relaxed, tranquil and in control. Nobody can enter this special place without your permission, so it is a place where you always have control.

In your special place, in your mind and in your imagination look all around you and do as much of the following as you can. Picture what you see. Touch something, hold it in your hand or brush your hand through it. Then hear what you hear, maybe the sound of birds singing, waves lapping against the shore or the gentle sound of running water. Now feel what you feel, it could be the warmth of the sun on your skin, or something else that arouses really pleasant feelings within you. Next aroma, smell something really pleasing, the scent of a flower or fresh air, anything that is pleasing to breath in through your nose and into your body. Finally use your sense of taste. You could imagine picking some fruit or berries, or eating something you particularly enjoy. Get in touch and involved with as many of your senses as you can.

Now think of the most relaxed thing you could ever think of, so you can let any cares, worries, stress, tension, anxiety or fear just fade away like a burden being released from your shoulders.

Perhaps you wouldn't mind me making some suggestions. You could be a feather blowing in the breeze, or blossom floating in the air, or maybe a tropical fish swimming around a coral reef, perhaps a soft fluffy white cloud drifting in the sky, (or whatever your own imagination indicates to you is the most relaxing thing you could ever imagine yourself being). What a comforting thought that is!

So now imagine yourself as the most relaxed thing you can think of. Then why not feel yourself floating up, or floating along, or floating down into a much deeper level of relaxation, because it is such a pleasant feeling to be so relaxed, that at the moment you're just not worried about anything. So you drift and float quite securely and happily within yourself.

Once you have practised this relaxation process a few times you will be able to do it relatively quickly.

The Subconscious Mind Exercise

Now having familiarised yourself with the elements 'Breathing,' The Count' and 'Creating your special place,' close your eyes and go through the process in your mind.

Take your time to do this until you are completely relaxed. Stay in this very relaxed state for a while. Then count from 1 to 10 and slowly bring yourself back to full-awakened consciousness and open your eyes feeling alert refreshed and invigorated.

Please remember when doing the subconscious mind exercises throughout this book, it is not necessary to go through the precise written text, relating to each exercise, word by word. Get in your mind the general essence and sequence of the ideas suggested and then go with the flow. Create your own experience. Do it your way, for your way is always the best for you.

NB. *Please remember - Because* **of the relaxation element in the subconscious mind exercises, they should** never **be carried out when** *you need to stay alert for some reason.*

The Whale

Whales have been roaming the oceans of the world for millions of years, long before man appeared on earth. As whales are mammals and have to breathe air to survive, they believed they had always to be near the surface of the ocean.

That was okay, except when storms, gales and hurricanes swept across the surface of the oceans and made it a place of discomfort and danger. It was not, in those circumstances, a favourable place to be. So the whales, being the wisest of creatures, soon learnt that if they controlled their breathing they were able to dive to great depths, away from the storms and discomfort at the surface. They developed elegant and effective ways of communicating with their mind and body and learnt to go deep down away from the dangers and stress at the surface.

They knew they could always return to the surface to breathe and seek nourishment and whatever else they needed from the environment without.

So with practice they were able to dive deeper and deeper into calm, deeper and deeper into relaxation, and deeper and deeper into tranquillity.

Although they knew they had to be at the surface to live and breathe, they also knew, to obtain protection, peace and tranquillity from the storms that often raged on the surface it was far better to go down within, where all could be peace and quiet. There they could be so much more in control of this environment than the stormy one above and when you're in control of the environment within, it is so much easier to be in control of the environment without.

So the whales practised this breathing control, time and time again. They found that with persistence of purpose, peace and comfort became automatic.

Relaxing deeply became a part of their everyday life and so it was then, now and ever after.

So when you practice profound relaxation on a daily basis, you'll enjoy a real sense of achievement, comfort, peace and control.

CHAPTER FIVE: THE MENTAL LAWS OF SUCCESS

The mental laws quoted in this book are 'laws' of the mind that have been widely quoted and used in general psychology and other 'talking therapies' for many years. It is not claimed they are based on scientific principles, such as the law of gravity for example; or have been verified by any formal medical research. They are essentially 'mind tools,' which when used constantly and effectively can help people to change in many positive ways. These laws essentially underpin chapters 6-11 in this book and will be introduced again in each respective chapter.

The Mental Law of Self-Awareness

For our self-development, this law suggests we need first to discover our essential nature and know who we really are. This knowledge of self can then provide a foundation for achieving what we want in life, both in respect of ourselves and in the wider world around us.

The knowledge of self-awareness is first and foremost a process of discovery until you get to the heart of the essential you.

It is of very little use to just journey through life, with your mind too frequently spinning around like a top. Just existing and not really living, going through the motions without those most important basic questions being answered.

How do I want to change, progress and develop?
What do I really want to achieve in my life?

The tendency is to drift along, without the basic knowledge of really knowing yourself as a person, just glossing over your dreams and aspirations. You believe you can't become the person you really want to be, or achieve what you really want out of life. You may never even get started, often using self-created barriers and obstacles, such as 'it's too late to change', or 'it's too difficult to change.'

> **With self- awareness you can close the gap between what you believe now and your potential for the future, rather than drifting along in the same old way.**

The first step on the pathway to a more successful, happy and fulfilled life is awareness of where you are in your life now and asking the questions.

What is going on in my life now?

In what ways do I want to change to meet my own personal needs?

Chapter 6 in this book encourages clarity of thinking in the self-awareness process, instead of spinning around from dawn to dusk, normally without a moment to spare, just existing and doing little more than that.

How curious will you be in finding out and realising that incorrect perceptions about your beliefs and behaviour can be changed into genuine beliefs that reflect the real you?

The Mental Law of Cause and Effect.

The law of cause and effect indicates, 'for every effect in our lives, there is a specific cause.'

You have the ability to control the causes and change the effects. Your thoughts are the primary cause of the conditions or effects in your life, and if you want your life to be different in the future, you have to change your thinking in the present.

Negative mind chatter is all about cause and effect. Professionals who are involved in the 'talking therapies' know when dealing with the human mind, the thoughts that go through our mind, from the day we are born, actually create the person we become.

Your inner dialogue is very relevant to your personal development and beliefs. You have the ability to control the causes and change the effects of anything you want because your thoughts are the principal causes of the conditions that affect your life.

Life doesn't need to be a lottery. If you want to change your behaviour and actions in the future, the only effective way to do this is to change your thinking in the present. Every thought you have generates an energy that turns your thoughts into your actions and behaviour.

One of the most damaging behaviours to engage in, causing a barrier to a life of enjoyment, happiness and success, is constant negative inner dialogue. Like everybody else you engage in inner mind dialogue. However, when it is mostly negative about you, others and the world in general, inner happiness becomes difficult to achieve. Chapter 7 deals with handling your negative dialogue by positive and effective use of your mind. When you really begin to notice how important it is to control negative mind chatter, you will be firmly on the pathway of change.

When your mind chatter is in the main negative then you live a mainly negative life. When your inner dialogue is predominantly positive then you live essentially a positive life. Your inner dialogue forms the focus of your feelings and your beliefs about yourself as a person and thus becomes the focus of your inner world.

The focus of your feelings and your beliefs become the reality by which you live. When you see a bright future for you, and change your focus, you make the majority of your thoughts positive. You will then change your life forever.

> **Imagine how your life would change when you take control of your negative mind chatter and change it into positive empowering inner dialogue.**

The Mental Law of Belief

The mental law of belief suggests that: "Whatever we believe with feeling and desire becomes our reality."

Your beliefs form a screen through which you observe the entire world and you never let any information that is inconsistent with your beliefs pass through the screen. Even if you have beliefs that are totally inconsistent with reality, because you believe them to be true, they become true for you. This idea is developed in chapter 8.

How would you feel if you knew that the negativity you believed about yourself wasn't true?

The thoughts you have held in your mind in the past have made you the person you are now. The thoughts you hold in your mind now, will make you the person you become in the future. You easily realise how that is logical and makes a whole lot of good sense. You are a reflection of your daily thoughts; you become what you think about every minute of the day.

It is very important that what you believe about you is true and valid because, accept it or not, what you believe about you, in many cases is not true. It is just the result of the way your mind has been influenced as you grew up, from an infant into an adult. That is why it is crucial to examine your beliefs.

Is what you believe about yourself really true?

The oft quoted saying of Henry Ford, the famous American industrialist, who had the courage and conviction to believe that automation would work and be successful, stated:

"If you think you can, or you think you can't, you are absolutely right."

That means if you really want to do something you will find a way to do it. If you think you can't do it you will just look for reasons to prove that it is impossible for you to do. Your thought processes actually dictate your response.

The confidence of self-belief is the cornerstone of achieving personal happiness and success. Leave in the past what belongs in the past and step along your future pathway with confidence to be yourself - every step empowering your feelings of self-worth and self-respect. You can be assured that, with genuine self-belief you can create a self-image that encourages change and success in everything you do.

By the time you have started to really believe in yourself, you'll be changing in ways you may have never thought possible and more quickly than you might have ever imagined.

The Mental Law of Control

The mental law of control indicates that we feel good about ourselves to the degree to which we are in control of our lives, and that we feel out of harmony with ourselves to the degree to which we feel we are controlled by circumstances or by other people.

One of the ways you can control your life is to seek the abundance of what you need in your life.

When my work in the commercial world became routine and mechanical, when I was just going through the motions, I dug down deep and found out what it was that I loved about the job in the first place. What drew me to it? What obsessed me about it? Then I realised how the job had changed. The fundamental reason became very clear. I was disillusioned with the way the business world was developing and it didn't suit me. I then thought about what I needed in my life now. I changed the course of my life completely and started, after professional training, my own private practice as a stress therapist The personal abundance I desired then manifested itself to me through the work I have done for many years involved in the 'talking therapies.' This has brought to me the abundance of happiness, success and fulfilment I desired.

If I had continued my attachment to my previous career in the commercial world, and all that was involved in my life then, I would never have gone down the new pathway I did - of that I am absolutely certain. It has not given me the monetary wealth I obtained in my commercial career but it has certainly given me the abundance I needed. It gave me control of my life in a way I had not previously experienced.

> **Have you ever considered you are too often chasing symbols that are more society's ideas of abundance than your own genuine individual desire?**

Some of the most insecure and unhappy people in this world are those who have all the symbols of society's idea of abundance. Unfortunately this material abundance comes and goes. Society is always changing its status symbols. So as soon as you have the current ones they become obsolete and you need other material things as the new symbols of abundance are established. It is entirely transitory, so it is always wise to be aware of mistaking society's symbols of abundance for those that are best suited to you. You can never have control of your life just by chasing after society's symbols of success.

> **Find out what you really want and obtain it, that's where real control of your life lies.**

With society's idea of abundance there is very little real choice of any genuine worth at all. It is just a continuous roundabout of consumerism and very little else. Why not move away from material stereotypes and control your life in a way that is right for you? Abundance is covered in greater detail in chapter 9.

Everything in life can be achieved more easily, not by struggle or fight, but by persistence of purpose, being in control and focused on what you desire.

The Mental Law of Attraction

The 'mental law of attraction' indicates that 'whatever a person allows to persistently stay in their mind with conviction and belief, they can manifest into their life.'

Like every other person, you radiate 'thought energy' and you invariably attract into your life the people and circumstances that harmonise with your dominant thoughts. If you want to attract different people, different circumstances and different events, you have to change the content of your thoughts. You can dramatically improve the quality of your life by taking control of your mind and creating beliefs and expectations consistent with what you desire.

The persistent use of the 'mental law of attraction' in your life can be used to activate a powerful method of self-improvement and self-actualisation to become the person you really want to be.

> **Focus persistently on the things you want and not on the things you don't want.**

If you focus on the person you want to be, on how you want to feel, how you want to behave and what you want to achieve and you do it with belief and conviction, then the 'law of attraction' will attract those things to you. 'The law of attraction', if used with conviction and belief, works effectively. If you dwell on your perceived limitations, frequently think thoughts of anxiety, fear and negativity, those are the things you will attract into your life.

Dwell on success, courage, empowerment, confidence, good health, balance and harmony as well as self-worth and self-respect and the "I can do it attitude." You then attract positive experiences into your life. Chapter 9 explains in detail how the 'law of attraction' can be brought positively into your life.

'The law of attraction' can be a difficult concept for many people to put into practice.

Do you often feel anxious and fearful?

Do you manifest anxiety, fear and stress in many aspects of your life?

You want to do something about it. You want to help yourself. However, as long as you dwell on fear, anxiety and all the things you perceive are wrong with yourself and your life, you just keep planting new seeds of negativity. You are then acting like a person who has planted some seeds and every few minutes goes out and stirs the earth to see if the seeds are growing. Negative thoughts and feelings do exactly this. They disturb the seeds of positive thoughts, such as confidence and courage and above all, self-esteem. Under such circumstances your positive seeds of thought can never grow. They are disturbed too often by negative thoughts - this is exactly what many of us do in our mental world.

To succeed in life it is important to plant your seeds of positive thought and leave them undisturbed. All it takes is persistence of purpose until you achieve what **you** want to achieve. Your positive seeds germinate, grow and flourish because you are using the law of attraction in support of you, instead of against you. Do it, believe it. As you believe, so it will happen. The seeds of happiness, success and fulfilment are not to be found in the, often superficial, world around you but deep within you.

As you sow positive thoughts in your mind it helps achieve that feeling deep inside of confidence and self-esteem, that you just know is there and cannot be disturbed or unsettled in any significant way.

You will know when you are doing it right because you will feel something like freedom, security, peace and contentment.

The Mental Law of Expectation

This law proposes that whatever we expect to happen with conviction and belief, either positive or negative, generally does happen.

'The mental law of expectation' is a powerful concept that suggests whatever you confidently expect in respect of your own performance becomes your self-fulfilling prophecy. You can enjoy high levels of accomplishment by continually talking to and about yourself as though you expect things to work out well. Expectations have a powerful impact on your relationships with others, and they have a powerful impact on the person you become. Chapters 10 and 11 encourage you to use the 'law of expectation' in many beneficial ways. People who enjoy high levels of accomplishment are continually using positive inner dialogue and internal imagery to create successful beliefs.

There are two key types of expectations that affect your life. First, the expectations your parents and other significant adults had of you in your childhood have a dramatic effect on how you perform as an adult. Second and most important are the expectations you have of yourself. They have a very powerful effect on your life.

You can change your expectations by putting into practice all you learn in this book. You can make effective changes in the way you feel and behave when you encourage positive expectations in every aspect of your life and really believe in you. Do you really accept that whatever beliefs you have held about yourself in the past have made you into the person you are now, and the beliefs you hold about yourself now will create the person you will be for all your tomorrows? When you do, you know you can change because whatever you persistently hold in your mind with belief and conviction, you can manifest into your life. **Neuroscience acknowledges that whatever you dwell on you embed deeper into your mind.** You can imagine what that means, *well can't you?* When you create the person you really want to be, you will know it is true.

Influencing your life can now be your most useful skill. When you realise this you will be amazed to discover how quickly your skill in influencing your thoughts and behaviour positively increases until you become the person you really want to be.

What you believe about yourself today dictates how you will be tomorrow. What you have created as your beliefs in the past, have made you the person you are in the present. If you change your beliefs you change you! Again, examine what you believe about you.

> **Change the negative beliefs about you that are wrong.**

You will discover there are many more positive things about you than you ever realised.

It is the genuine belief that brings your desires to fruition. Focus on the what, and the how will be taken care of. This doesn't mean you will not have to do anything. Of course you will. But when you relax, let go of the anticipated results and trust your own subconscious mind to guide you along the right pathway for you, your life can be entirely different from what it has been in the past.

CHAPTER SIX: SELF-AWARENESS

I suggest at this point you revisit chapter 5, pages 45-46 and read again –'The Mental Law of Self-Awareness,' which underpins the content of this chapter.

We all have behavioural and emotional challenges but what we often do is try to pretend they don't exist, or we run away from them or ignore them in some other way. It's only the most courageous amongst us who are willing to submit ourselves to the difficult process of self-examination; they are the bravest of all.

The more awareness you have about yourself, the more options you allow yourself to look at, the more flexible you become. You can also start to accept and understand other people's points of view more easily. You can understand that everybody is right from his or her perspective. You can learn to respect other people's views, even if you disagree with them. You can then allow others to be who they want to be and accept they are not always going to act and behave as you expect.

It's critical for you to be realistic, to have a true knowledge of yourself as you are, and to recognise both the good and the bad parts of yourself. The capacity for ongoing change and self-development is crucial on your pathway to personal happiness.

How often do you move through life at high speed and fail to notice your own personal needs, like a hamster spinning around on its wheel, getting nowhere fast?

It is true if you are endlessly dashing about you can achieve a great deal, however as a result the quality of your life is often poor.

Do you often find in the fast moving electronic dominated world you live in, you are reluctant to just sit down and think, and ask,' what is my life all about?'

Do You Value Your Life?

It is so easy for you to be hurrying about all the time, being unaware of your real needs, or showing compassion for yourself. Awareness is very difficult when you are perpetually on the 'hamster wheel of life,' what will you do if you fall off the wheel? You can't worry or busy your way to happiness!

So with a daily dose of fear from…

- being told what you lack or need by advertisers and…
- the government and/society in general telling you, what you should or should not do, and…
- the media constantly reporting seemingly endless negative news…

…it's not surprising that you can feel disconnected from your real self.

That's a choice of course. That's one way to live life, with all that anxiety fear and worry. You can obtain material wealth, but you cannot achieve happiness and fulfilment just from money, or by jetting around the world for a holiday once or twice a year. So when you are battling with stress and anxiety, when you are striving for balance within your high-speed life, maybe the issue is slowing down and devoting some part of your life, each day, just for you, your own needs, and your own desires. Why not become your own best friend. *Ever thought of being that? Well, have you?*

When you quieten your mind, listen and wait, the truth has a way of revealing itself. You will find that negative habits, behaviour, stress and anxiety can be changed to peace and control.

Is your life often painful? It is wise never to be fooled by illusions or false perceptions. Pain whether physical or mental is an indication for you to change, it forewarns you that something is wrong and you would be wise to take notice of it.

Asking The Right Questions

What stops you pondering on your life at deeper levels of consciousness? Asking yourself...

- *"What is it going to take for me to slow down sometimes?*
- *What would it be like to have some profound peace in my life, how do I manage that?*

- *How can I pull the lever back during my day and slow up?*
- *How would it be to breathe with awareness and relax and take in the pleasure and the sensations of just being me?"*

The more self-awareness you have, the greater the relationship with yourself you have, and being in a world in which you can say:

- I don't have to criticise myself just because I didn't know, I just made a mistake and it didn't go how I wanted it to. That isn't the time for putting myself down but time to ask: "what can I learn from all this? How can I do it differently next time?"

Has it ever occurred to you that with the power of your own mind you can heal emotional scars and use your natural skills and resources to do so?

> **You can use feelings and internal imagery to change in positive ways and, more than that, it is relatively easy to do when you know how.**

When you hold yourself up to impossible standards of living, when you hold up perfection as the only way you should be, when you hold up living in a society that doesn't value self-care and only believes that if you don't win, you have failed, then you are accepting society's 'game rules'. When you push through the day and do not include your own needs, do not include your own aspirations and ignore the messages your mind and body are sending to you as to what you need for rest and replenishment, then you're affirming your world is a world of punishment. Therefore you go endlessly through all that you must do, need to do, have to do, should do and ought to do.

> **Mistakes are only experiences to learn from, just do things differently in the future.**

It's all about continuing to move on your journey through life in a more loving and compassionate way towards yourself, towards being the real you, your own personal fulfilment.

You know if you go on doing the same old things you get the same old results. I am not going to say you need to change because that's a decision you have to make for yourself.

Do you agree that it would be worthwhile if you focused on these questions?

- *"What do I need to do to be the person I want to be?*
- *What do I need to change?"*

Why not become more and more curious about the opportunities that surround you, instead of feeling insecure and having doubts about yourself.

> **Be your true self and attract automatically to yourself the things that make you feel good, that feel right for you.**

In the past, in an effort to cope with life, you have probably put a lot of will power and effort in an attempt to change your negative emotions and behaviour, with very little reward. By following the advice and guidance offered in this book and using your mind in the ways suggested, you will find it much easier and certainly more rewarding than the previous way of wasting your mind energy and creating stress. This process begins when you start using the 'Subconscious Mind Exercise' at the end of this chapter. Always appreciate that in using your mind to achieve change, persistence of purpose is important.

Taking responsibility for the self is the key to change. It means you don't leave a trail of emotional baggage you haven't dealt with that tends to follow you into the present and future. It's this baggage that prevents you from developing your life.

You are probably aware of the fact that life is frequently not the way you think it should be. Things aren't supposed to be easy, just possible. So if you were to cast your mind back, as far as it needs to go and remember something you've done that you found difficult at first but with which, by persevering, you succeeded in the long run. There are no doubt many such situations, they all add up to realising how you can keep going and how you can remain open to learning from a difficulty or anything that is not working in your life and do it better next time.

You never help yourself by thinking, "I am stupid, I am silly" and similar negative thinking. When you create a stress response, you create a chemical, which in excess breaks down body tissue and depletes the immune system. When you produce too much of this chemical through too much stress, anxiety and worry, from too much fight, from too much self-attack, in due course this can make you feel depressed and anxious. You can then wonder.

"Why am I like this?"

When you are not at peace with yourself, it means you are not accepting your feelings. Accept first, release any stress and anxiety, then change how you're feeling. You will start doing this automatically as you introduce effective positive thinking into your life. As this happens you're going to laugh your head off - when you find out how much fun you have, being the new you. You give yourself time to discover the essential you, because that's always interesting to do.

By following the guidance in this chapter, you can learn, at deeper levels of consciousness, ways of becoming more self-aware and realise there are many ways to increase opportunities in your life, possibilities that surround you all the time.

> **We all change. The question is, do we direct the change or just let change happen in a haphazard way.**

You are probably really frustrated with all the ways you have tried to heal emotional challenges with quick fix methods. Truthfully, using the power of your own mind is the only really worthwhile way, certainly the only way that lasts. So sit down quietly, no longer on the 'hamster wheel, 'contemplating on...

- *"how do I make it all work for me?*
- *how can I live my life, from my beliefs?*

"If I am not living my life according to my own beliefs and too often doing and saying things because other people feel it is right to act in a certain way, then I am not living with integrity within myself. It is hard for my mind and body to stay in balance and harmony unless I have self-respect, self-worth and self- belief in and for me."

Like many other people who succeed in their daily work you can gain material wealth but...

Do you forget about your own personal needs? Do you just carry on regardless and not allow yourself to get off the 'hamster wheel' long enough to consider what your life is all about?

Maybe you don't make a commitment to yourself, only to what others and society expect of you. However, there is another more important need, beyond material success: the emotional needs of the self. True happiness comes from being true to one's self. It is easy when you know how.

Well, isn't believing that better than keep saying to yourself "I can't change?"

How about believing the time to change is now?

Why not learn to understand with your feelings. When you are upset, frustrated or angry, get to know what is happening in your body and mind.

If you simply agree to what life is, there's a deep relaxation that happens and all of a sudden you stop fighting yourself. The issues, the challenges around habits and behaviour, take on a different light and you don't need excuses any more to do what you know is right for you.

It's nice to know what is right for you, so if you would like to know, you can ask yourself these questions.

- *"Am I happy to be here with all that my life is now?*
- *Have I settled all my past emotional baggage and left behind all I considered negative and unhelpful?"*

It doesn't mean you have to accept every part of your past as if everything was acceptable. Simply agree that it's occurred, that it's happened and what's more you have survived. If you haven't agreed fully then ask yourself:

"What would it take for me to come to terms with all in my past I haven't dealt with and leave it in the past where it belongs?"

Decide what you want to do now. Ask yourself:

"What do I want to do now?"

Then just notice how those thoughts impact on your relationship with you now, and what you want to change now.

You can empower yourself to change by simply expressing the truth of who you really are. Saying the things you want to say. Being the person you want to be. Stepping into your place in the world and doing what you want to do.

When you are not claiming your own personal power you are denying your true needs. From this mindset it is easy to reach for the quick fix but that actually drains your power to change. You need intention to change; if the intention is absent change will not happen.

You can avoid the truth in the fear it might jolt you out of your cosy but precarious safety zone. You can avoid change. The quick fix is so much easier, well so it can seem.

Ponder on these...

- *"What are the truths I am withholding from me?*
- *What are the truths I have inside me that are calling me to seek change.*

Positive thinking

Live with enthusiasm and an 'I can do it mentality,' which is the springboard of all personal success. Feel confidence building up inside you, like a powerful beam of light, surging through every cell of your body, into your very being.

Trying doesn't work. Succeed instead! What you focus on increases. If you have never realised this before, you do now.

> **Your life can be enormously improved by doing less.**

The secret is not to do less of everything but to do less of those things that don't work very well for you, and do more of the things that deliver what you want in your life.

Why not move away from just doing everything in a haphazard way, so many things that lead to disappointing results, making things worse than they already are. You know all about the mass of trivia that constantly surrounds you and has a tendency to engulf your life. You know all about…

have to,
must do,
need to do,
ought to do,
should do
and all that old negative stuff. *Well, don't you?*

The following is one of the most important truths about life that allows a person to change and live their life from a basis of genuine self-esteem rather than in a state of stress and anxiety.

Many years ago Eleanor Roosevelt wife of the famous president of the U.S.A, said:

"Nobody can hurt you unless you allow him or her to do so."

> **It is not people, things, experiences or situations that cause us stress and anxiety but the view and perceptions we take of them.**

(The above truism is of intrinsic importance for any person to become the person they really want to be). ***If you really understand the truth of this you can change your life in amazing ways.***

Working Positively With Your Subconscious Mind

We all know that 'reading' and 'doing' are two very different things. So the following subconscious mind exercise, if you are persistent with it, will enable you to start putting into practice the changes you want to make.

Now create in your mind how you want to be in the future. Start focusing on these important changes…

1. Those things that you believe will work well for you - bring them into your imagination, along with the positive feelings they give you;
2. Changes that will bring you happiness, success and fulfilment.

Always dwell on how you want to change, feel and behave. This is of vital importance in your ability to achieve what you want in your life. You must always show your subconscious how you want it to help you change by using clear positive inner dialogue words and imagery.

Once you have decided the changes you want to make about your life, write them down so they are in a form you can easily refer to. Always write in the positive. Never write I don't want to be like this or like that, write clearly how you want to be.

Your time is very valuable, so wouldn't it be useful to do far fewer of the trivial things and focus much more on what you want in life? Why not keep that image permanently in your mind, so your subconscious mind can assist you in moving towards it in a supportive way, helping you to bring it ever closer and place it definitely in your 'future' now.

Then allow your subconscious mind to choose the most important change you really want to make. Focus on it. Notice how you are thinking and behaving and what you are doing as if this change has already happened. How you are feeling! How you are behaving! How you are speaking! How it really feels to be **you** with this change already accomplished. As you become at one with this image, see yourself clearly in your mind's eye.

What is happening? What are you doing? How does it feel?

Feel all the emotions, and all the sensations.

Focus on how your life is now and how it is going to change. Then build a bridge that you can cross. You really want to be different in the future. *Well don't you?* You have now established the new patterns. Now you can be that new person. Have more confidence in who you are and where you are going. Now you can bounce back when things don't go as planned, maintaining your integrity, focusing on solutions and not on perceived obstacles. Seize each moment positively.

The Subconscious Mind Exercise

When you quieten yourself down, even if only for five minutes or so you can find there is a place in yourself where you exist that is not the endless chatter that is going on in your mind – that is not your body – is not you physically, but is a place where you just are, where there is a different kind of consciousness. This is where positive change can be made.

Having decided on the changes you want to make about yourself close your eyes and go through the relaxation process in chapter 4, pages 37-40, you have already familiarised yourself with.

This way of relaxing soon becomes very easy for you. So after a while it only takes a few minutes to do, but always take as much time as you need, to go deep down inside and shut out the world around you.

Now focus fully on the most important changes you want to make, one at a time, and for each change see yourself, in your imagination, as the person you want to be in every respect and behaving in situations as you want to. Do this from time to time throughout each day and as you fall asleep at night. It is a very powerful way to start you along the pathway of becoming the person you really want to be. You have to learn to adjust through time before the true gifts of success are achieved. When visualising the future you want, don't analyse what you are creating in your mind, just do it.

NB. *Please remember* – **Because of the relaxation element in the subconscious mind exercises, they should <u>never</u> be done when** *you need to stay alert*

Looking Towards a Positive Future.

You have faced many challenges in your life. The time has now come for you to meet the greatest challenge of all. You have started on your own personal pathway towards a life of success, **true** happiness and fulfilment, to do and achieve all those things about you personally, that you have left 'on the burner' just simmering away for far too long.

Wherever you are in your life now, there are many more possibilities than you might have ever imagined. There is more you are capable of achieving, more you are meant to do, experience and enjoy in fulfilling your personal desires and dreams. Few people realise the full extent of their potential. You can if you have the determination and belief to do so.

As you go through this book you can gently and surely tap into the potential within, into your deepest reserves of the creative you and move persistently forward, to the abundance life can offer and the personal fulfilment you have always yearned for.

> **The truth is you only achieve personal success, happiness and fulfilment if you do it your way, for your way is always the best way for you.**

Success and true happiness in life depends on mental conditioning. That means guiding your life, your way and in a way that you know is right for you. Not what anybody else or society says is right for you.

This book provides you with the necessary 'mental scaffolding' to build your life, your way, because only **you know** what success and happiness means to **you.** This book can help you to identify the basic mental resources you need to create your own particular pathway to the success and happiness you desire.

READ ON AND ACHIEVE IT.

<u>**You will notice as you progress through this book that some concepts and ideas are repeated; this is because it is a positive way by which the mind effectively works and learns. Repetition enables us to engage with important concepts time and time again, which means it integrates new understandings into our mind in an easy and effortless way.**</u>

Your Journey of Discovery

In using your mind to absorb the ideas and suggestions contained in this book, you are on a voyage of discovery and realising a new journey takes longer getting there than coming back, or making the journey again.

If you go the average way, or even the longer way you still get there just the same. What's important is you go the right way for you, knowing if you do all the things necessary for success, with persistence of purpose, you will arrive where you desire to be.

Always moving ahead in a calm and relaxed way, resting at times to consider and contemplate as you go along, continuing steadily forward step by step. Being too quick can mean you complete your journey too soon, before all is ready or prepared, for a successful arrival.

You can always go back somewhere and then go forward again, as it is always easier to go back over a journey you have already experienced once before. With each step you are going through a process that brings you nearer and nearer to the goals you have set yourself and the things you want to achieve.

You can also make mistakes and change them into challenges, with the full knowledge that this or that part of the journey can be revisited to check and reassess, whenever that maybe required. Positive progress is always made as it occurs, in perspective and in accordance with your own particular needs and requirements.

You have all the resources you require. All you need to learn is how to resource *change* to get hold of and use those resources. So many changes you desire are made along the way, often imperceptibly, with effortless intention, because everyone has their own way and that is always the best way for them.

However you also understand and appreciate, you can't really know something and or take the fullest advantage of it until you have practiced every piece of it thoroughly.

One of the most important changes you can make on your journey is not only discovering new landscape but also using your eyes, ears and imagination in ways that enable you to see the old landscape differently. *Well isn't that encouraging to know?*

CHAPTER SEVEN: NEGATIVE INNER DIALOGUE

The 'Law of Cause and Effect' suggests that every thought is a real energy force and therefore it has to create something. This can either cause negative or positive feelings. Every moment of your life and everything you experience in your life is created by energy. You can use your personal energy negatively or positively. What you will be doing reading this book and carrying out the subconscious mind exercises, will involve the positive use of your own mind energy to achieve the changes you want to make about yourself.

Thoughts are energy and can be scientifically measured. That means you cannot have a thought without it having an effect, without something happening. The thought is the cause and the feeling produced is the outcome of the thought. Your mind and body works by the creation of energy. The secret is to direct your energy positively to create the changes you desire.

The information and exercises in this book will help you use your personal energy to aid your psychological well-being. You will learn to tune and focus it and direct it whenever and wherever you desire. You will be able to control and change your subconscious thinking instead of allowing it to control you negatively.

> **Just imagine in the days and weeks ahead being able to control and release stress and anxiety, as easily as breathing in and out, and how that changes your life in a positive way.**

Anxiety is a natural human given that all people experience. It is very useful when you are faced with a real danger, like being confronted by a vicious animal or walking too near the edge of a cliff on a very windy day. It is protective to experience it in those circumstances. However when anxiety occurs in situations when it is irrational to do so, then it is not needed or wanted, *wouldn't you agree?*

The self-talk you engage in is one of the most crucial factors in assisting you to create the successful future you desire. Your inner dialogue generally referred to as mind chatter, whether it is predominantly positive or negative, dictates how you perform as a person - whether you are in a state of anxiety or in control.

Have you used self-talk to disguise reality from yourself?

It is a very human trait because in your mind, when you do this, you can absolve yourself from personal responsibility.

Have you ever said any of the following?

- "It isn't my fault.
- Nothing has gone right for me since that happened.
- I can't do anything about it.
- It's the government's fault.
- It's the local council's fault.
- I didn't do it; it just happened, it wasn't my fault.
- It's my boss's fault, or it's the company's fault.
- All the things I do always go wrong.
- He/she stresses me out."

Have you ever generalised like this to blame your lack of success on some global bad luck or even a curse you were convinced was upon you and outside your power to change. How often do you say?

- "It was his fault.
- It was her fault.
- It was their fault,"

Our excuses can be unendingly creative.

You can so easily get in the habit of using negative thinking to distance yourself from personal responsibility and believe life in general is against you. This can be done with the conscious mind. However it never succeeds in quite the same way with your subconscious mind. Self-deluding talk never helps you to develop and progress your life. It roots you in the past and prevents you moving positively into the future.

What you essentially say with negative self-talk is, "I can't really do anything about it, and so I have to stay as I am"- thus turning you into a victim, rather than accepting you're responsible for your own thoughts and actions.

I am reminded of the time my Granddaughter Ella when she was 3 years old said to her brother Zach, when he made a nasty remark about her...

"I'm making myself hurt about what you said to me Zach."

She didn't blame it onto her brother, in some childlike wise way she accepted it was her feelings that caused the hurt. However, as children grow up they start to learn how to manipulate language and instead of saying "I hurt myself," it is turned into "it's your fault I feel like this." Then as adults we get expert at shifting personal responsibility from ourselves to others. We have all been there. It's so easy to do.

The first thing to do when you want to progress and develop your life in a positive way is to say and believe, "whatever has happened to me, I am responsible for my life **now**." How to deal with painful and hurtful experiences that have happened to you in the past is to release them and the rest of this chapter gives guidance on how you can do that.

Positive self-talk focuses your attention on how you really want to be and your mind automatically focuses on that. If however your inner talk is negative and you are, focusing on how you don't want to be, your mind will focus on that, just as easily.

> **Remember whatever you allow to persistently dwell in your mind with belief and conviction, you can also manifest into your life.**

You either create positive expectations or negative ones in accordance with the constant inner dialogue you have with yourself. Yes it is as simple as that; positive mind chatter empowers you to succeed. Negative chatter focuses you on how you don't want to be. Much of the negative stuff is about the past anyway. What is the use of going over all that, time and time again?

Haven't you had enough of that already? Well haven't you?

Blaming others for what happens to you is never productive, even if there is some just cause to do so.

Do you realise the crucial role negative mind chatter plays in stress and anxiety? Everybody to some degree engages in negative inner dialogue. Controlling this negative chatter is a vital part of releasing unnecessary stress and anxiety. As you suddenly start controlling it you will discover how true this is.

Why not choose to start letting go of all the daily external forces that are normally part of your life, the things that weigh you down and the things that hang heavily on your shoulders? Why not let go of all that kind of thinking.

The guidance in this chapter is starting a process that will empower you to release negative mind chatter. When you do this you leave much more room for positive mind talk. That means you can use the majority of your mind for learning how to think positively. As you do this, your life will improve in ways you might never have thought possible.

> **Be aware of your internal mind chatter and keep changing it from negative to positive.**

You're going to prove to yourself how easily you can change unwanted feelings into desirable ones. So why not enjoy the comfort of breathing in deeply and letting it out slowly. Now think of a person or an experience or a thought that brings happiness and joy into your life. Imagine a safe space to be in with someone you love. It could even be some spiritual entity if your belief allows you to do that, or someone from your past that is no longer with you. Whatever brings you to a peaceful state of mind, it is important to avoid going down the path of sadness or regret.

You came into the world without a self-concept. Every concept of who you are you learned as you grew up. Negative input as a child can cause negative self-concepts. These can remain with you unless you start using your mind positively to create reality rather than disillusion in your life.

As a child you learnt from repetition, whether what you learnt was positive or negative, true or false, valid or invalid. You based what you believed as a child on your interpretation of what you repeatedly heard and the behaviour you repeatedly observed. Once your subconscious mind decides something is true it holds onto such beliefs very tenaciously, until it can be convinced what the true facts are. Be assured your subconscious mind can change otherwise you would stay in the same old negative trances forever.

Asking the Right Questions

Find something in those childhood times that disappointed you, that even angered you. It could have been something your parents or a sibling said, or somebody else said. Focus on that for a moment, hold it in your mind and be curious in a relaxed way.

Then ask yourself,
- *"am I still living that experience,*
- *did I judge myself because of that experience,*
- *did I allow that to alter my life by hanging on to it in a negative way?"*

If it still gives you pain or sadness *you* might want to deal with that experience and say goodbye to it. You can say:

"It no longer belongs to me," (Make sure you really mean it.) "It was just something that happened along the way, it is not of any relevance in my life now. There were many such events that happened throughout my life that happened along the way. I don't want them to be part of my life now."

Are there any negative experiences from the past that you use to judge yourself by or that you use to define yourself by?

Did someone say you were not good enough; did you ever not live up to someone's expectations of how you should be?

Why not take any such experience and say:
"It does not have any relevance for me now."
Ask…

- *"Is there anything I have learned from this, is this about who I am?*
- *Do I need this kind of thinking any more or is this just someone else's perception of me?"*

As a child you often accepted what was said about you was true. The younger you were the more you accepted it. As an adult you can still respond and react to the negative criticism of others in the same anxious way. So the question to ask is:

"Are they still affecting me now?

If they are, why not separate these experiences one at a time. Ask:

"Is the sadness it caused in my life still with me now?"

If it is, why not let go of it or whatever the situation was? Let it go, it is the past. Release it from your life now.

Do not allow yourself to be unjustly judged by others. As you go through these experiences, you can go through them in a new way, in a positive way. If you search thoroughly enough you can always learn something useful.

You clear all the old negativities from the past and leave them in the past where they belong. Then bring the process up to the current moment. Your subconscious mind can do this with a speed and clarity that your conscious mind is just incapable of doing. I don't know exactly how you will look at those past experiences now and ask:

- *"Do these thoughts matter now?*
- *Am I building my thoughts around these experiences now?*
- *Am I still searching for who I am in the eyes of others now?"*

If you find you are still doing these things why don't you simply let it all go and be the real you?

Then drift to your teenage years...

Is there something here that needs attention? Were you happy with yourself? Was there joy in your life?

If not, perhaps it would be beneficial to look at what caused you any pain.

If once again what is causing you pain is no longer relevant in your life now, it would benefit you to let it go, *well wouldn't it?* It would empower you to say:

"You do not have any influence over my life now.' I am who I am.

Nothing and no one or any thought situation or experience can hurt or harm me unless I allow it to"

Parent Relationships

Turn for a moment to your parents. What an ambivalent relationship we can have with them, especially in our teenage years, or even earlier, can't we just! Remember parents have 'feet of clay', like us all. They react to what they experienced in their childhood and do what seems right.

It is a requirement of your own personal development (and very advantageous) to let go of the perceptions and the pain of experiences from the past. You were a child who perceived your existence based on what people thought of you. If you let go now of what does not work for you, you allow space to create the real you, the person you actually are.

Why not accept your earlier years were a learning curve, during which your parents and other significant adults and peers only did what they thought was right however- wrong you felt it was? That is often painful to think about but you need to do it to clear away many of the old 'cobwebs' that are still cluttering up your life.

Dealing With Feelings

So why not experiment by changing hurtful feelings into pleasurable feelings? Experiment by doing the 'Exercises for Overcoming Negative Mind Chatter' on pages 82-84. Find out the exercise that works best for you. Your subconscious mind will then become aware of the kind of feelings you want to be dominant in your life. You don't have to allow the past to affect you in a negative way now. If you start to imagine how you will feel when you've let go of all that old negative stuff, you can really begin to realise how effectively you can change.

You do not need anyone's permission to be who you are. You are your own individual and unique person with vices and virtues like anybody else. When you really begin to accept yourself at a deep level, with all that has happened, either hurtful or pleasurable, you'll free yourself to change whatever you want to change. What a liberating feeling that will be. *How would you feel if you did that?* So bring your thoughts back to where you are in your life now and leave all the old negative baggage behind.

After you have gone through all that experimenting with your feelings and left those old invalid perceptions and fears behind where they belong, you will feel light and free. Remember to say to yourself repeatedly, when you feel you are falling into the old trap of negative thinking:

> **"Nothing and no one, or any thought, experience or situation, can harm or hurt me in any way unless I allow them to,"**

Most of what happens in respect of releasing negativity from the past will take place in your inner mind and you will not always be conscious of it. The changes can happen subconsciously but effectively.

However be aware of that old negative mind chatter if it returns. Be prepared to deal with it and say: "That was then, this is now" and really mean it. "I do not give negative mind chatter any more power."

If the mind chatter pops up again, say again these words:

"I do not give negative thoughts any more power, they do not have any place in my life anymore".

By the time you have started these statements the negative chatter is already going away. *Can you imagine how that will change your life?*

If the negative mind-chatter returns at any time be firm say "No! I have decided negativity does not have a place in my life any more. There isn't any place for negativity from the past in my life." Keep repeating these words as many times as you need. Remember the mind learns best by little changes that happen regularly, the same message repeated time and time again.

Therefore everything you say and everything you do rises above fear, doubt, or whatever negativity there may be. Remember to go back to that safe, quiet, special place inside. Remember what your intention is and find the resources you need which have been there all the time. Then the fear and doubt disappears. This is a step-by-step process and persistence of purpose encourages success.

When you really begin to believe that success is possible, everything becomes so much easier. You then find it easier and easier to succeed.

Successful people know that persistence of purpose is the way to be successful. If you at any time feel some particular negative mind chatter is persistent, just be more determined than ever to succeed. The challenge is to quieten the critic inside you, that little voice that so often in the past has generated fear and persuaded you that you couldn't achieve what you wanted to. When you engage in negative chatter there are some specific exercises you can do to eradicate effectively this negative self-talk.

If there is a persistent problem with the internal critic inside, you can fix it and fix it fast. You can learn the following exercises easily and do them at any time and in any place. People who do these exercises persistently know how simple and effective they are.

Exercises for overcoming negative mind chatter:

Controlled breathing - Breathe slowly and deeply and focus on your stomach as you breathe in and your chest as you breathe out. This simple but effective technique diverts attention from the negative dialogue to the breathing process and stops the thoughts going on and on.

Replace the negative chatter with positive self-talk by creating positive internal imagery. See and feel the negative thoughts float away as dark clouds drifting out of sight. Then replace them with good positive thoughts represented by fluffy white clouds in an azure blue sky, drifting gently towards you, bringing peace, tranquillity and positive thoughts

You can imagine the dialogue is on a CD and you have something to scratch the CD hard and thus eliminate the negative chatter. Then follow up with a new CD that contains alternative positive inner dialogue.

If you're a person who prefers to be very direct just shout "<u>Stop! Stop</u>," halt it in its tracks; have nothing to do with it. Take control whenever negative chatter tries to control you.

> You can also use your innate imaginative resources to go back to a time when you were happy and carefree, a time when you were having fun, or when you achieved something that gave you a feeling of accomplishment and satisfaction. Encourage positive feelings to flow through your whole body, wave after wave of peace, joy and the, <u>I can do it spirit</u> and just override those negative thoughts with good positive thoughts. Then make contact with the child in your heart and all those marvellous things you learnt as an infant, first sitting up and ending with running and jumping. It can open up that <u>I can do it</u> belief that you may think you have lost.
>
> If you are a conservationist why not create a spin machine. Then place any negative thoughts that stick in your mind into your spin machine turn the machine on and create enormous energy that spins the thought around at great speed so it recycles the negative energy into positive energy.

Whatever you choose to do, do something; don't just let negative thinking prattle on and on.

> **Controlling negative mind chatter is essential in becoming the person you want to.**

A number of exercises have been suggested so you <u>can choose what works for you.</u>

Once you have practiced these exercises for a while, you can even create ways of your own to deal with negative mind chatter. Wouldn't that be a fun and useful thing to do?

Subconscious Mind Exercise

Relax your mind and body as shown in chapter 4, pages 37-40. Then go back to your earlier days and bring to mind any hurtful events that occurred, particularly those concerning your parents or siblings and other members of your wider family. Work through these memories using the guidelines shown earlier in this chapter. If any of these negative events are still causing hurt in your life deal with them and leave them back in the past where they belong.

Be cautious but persistent when going through this exercise. You are dealing with some of the most important aspects of your life that have contributed to how you feel now. Go through this exercise many times until all the old hurts have been healed and you can progress your life without past negative events affecting your confidence and self-esteem.

Forgiveness is always an important element in healing hurtful past events. Read about the section headed forgiveness at the beginning of the next chapter in this book, pages 90-93. Really understand what forgiveness means in a therapeutic context. Remember you are healing these past situations for your own peace of mind. Keep this in mind all the time especially when you find any particular event difficult to resolve.

It is not an easy mind exercise to engage in but when you have successfully completed it and you have put all that past hurt behind you it will give you a great feeling of relief freedom and comfort.

NB. *Please remember* – **Because of the relaxation element in the subconscious mind exercises, they should <u>never</u> be done when *you need to stay alert***

CABINETS & DUSTBINS.

My old Nan said to me when I was a young boy, "You know Michael. I have created a way to store my good memories so I can recall them whenever I want to."

"Really Nan," I replied. "How do you do that?"

"Well I have a cabinet that I have created in my mind. It's the most wonderful cabinet I can possibly make. It's made of beautiful grained wood with a wonderful inlaid design and mother of pearl decoration. It's always wonderfully polished and clean. Of course people can make their own memory cabinet exactly how they want it to look and of the material they want it made and everything about it just right for them."

"My cabinet has many small drawers" my Nan continued, "and in each small draw I store a happy memory, or a special achievement of mine. When I first created my memory cabinet I thought about all the past good memories I had, and all my achievements and the positive things, however small and put each one of them in a drawer. As my cabinet is in my mind I can create as many drawers as I like. On each drawer I create a word, picture, or symbol that immediately brings back the memory to me, a quick sign of recognition as it were. In this way I was able to store all my good memories from the past. We all have them; however unhappy life may have been at times. I carefully placed each one in a drawer of my memory cabinet. Each time I brought back a good happy memory, or one of my achievements, I brought the positive feelings with it, the happiness, confidence and self-esteem all came back to me in the present."

Nan continued, "Whenever I have a new good experience, a happy experience, a special experience, I place it immediately in my memory cabinet should I forget it. We all know how easy it is to forget what was good and how we have the habit of hanging on to the bad experiences. I also mark any new happy memories with a word, picture, or symbol and there it is forever to recall all the joy of it. This means whenever I want them I always have many good memories to recall, to help me cope with times when life seems not so good, or even unhappy and sad. I also have a key to lock my cabinet which means nobody can ever steal any of my good memories from me."

"Whenever I feel depressed stressed or anxious, I take my key, go to my cabinet in my mind unlock those good memories and special achievements and dwell on them, all those happy good things in my life. For I know, **whatever I allow to dwell persistently in my mind becomes a part of my life** and isn't it so much better to dwell on that which is happy and joyous than that which is sad and depressive?"

I thought this was a really marvellous approach to life, to think of something that is really uplifting and cheerful and let it dwell in the mind, rather than what we so often do... dwell on that which is unsupportive or even downright miserable.

I then asked my Nan, "What do you do with the bad memories and unwanted thoughts and feelings, the hurtful memories or the occasions when you feel you haven't achieved that which you wanted to?"

"Oh those," she replied, "Well that's easy. I have an old rusty dustbin covered with cobwebs; it's a really horrible sight. I just dump all my bad hurtful memories in this old dustbin where they belong.

"I always go to it to throw away hurtful, unwanted thoughts and feelings. Otherwise I never think about it at all. I learn my lessons from any experiences that didn't go, as I desired them to, then throw the unwanted feelings into the dustbin and forget about them. They are no longer of any use to me whatsoever. Rubbish into a rubbish bin, that's the only place for them. I certainly don't want to allow this rubbish to clutter up my mind. However if I want to revisit a positive lesson from any bad experience, I can take it out the bin and examine it once more - but I never forget to put it back in the bin when I have dealt with it."

I think that is such a great way of dealing with life's ups and downs, whether they are great or small, because we all experience good positive memories and hurtful bad ones. If we treat the negative ones as rubbish, to be disposed of so they don't linger in our mind, we leave them in the past where they belong. The good ones we treasure and put them lovingly and carefully into our 'Cabinet of Treasured Memories' to be remembered and called upon whenever we want to.

During my many years as a professional therapist I really began to understand the significance of what my Nan said to me all those years ago. As a therapist I learnt very quickly that people were very persistent in keeping negative memories in their minds and forgetting their good memories. It appears to be a very common human trait. I realised what a wonderful idea my Nan had created as an example of positive thinking, and what an effective idea she had created in helping a person to cope with life; *what do you think?*

Create your own memory cabinet, arrange it how you want to and in a way that works for you.

CHAPTER EIGHT: SELF-BELIEF

The Mental Law of Belief is one of the most important of all the mental laws. Turn back to chapter 5, page 48-49 and read again the section on the 'law of self-belief' really appreciate the significance of what this law means.

As described in the previous chapter, the basic beliefs you have about yourself were formed in early childhood. Many of these beliefs are formed from what your parents or other significant adults and your peers said or did or more importantly, what you perceived the meaning was of what they said or did. This would be especially when they acted or behaved in a way that really hurt you.

It is always as well to remember that like us, parents do their best based on experiences of their childhood and their life in general. This is the same for all parents. However good or bad you feel your childhood experiences were, (for most of us it is somewhere in between), relationships with parents are usually, at least somewhat ambivalent.

It should be appreciated that most people do their best, they do what they feel is right - even those who act in ways you think are really bad. They still behave in a way they think is okay. This applies to all relationships - family, peer groups at school, colleagues at work and in social situations as well. What one person thinks is right can be very different from what another thinks is right. This is an important concept to accept when working on forgiveness

Forgiveness

One of the things we all have to do to build genuine feelings of self-belief is to ensure anything negative in our past has been positively dealt with. Brooding anger, simmering rage, jealousy, envy and self-pity are feelings that only poison and corrode the mind. It is far more beneficial to let it all go and allow forgiveness into your life, so your mind can tick along harmoniously and at peace. You can then keep all your thinking progressive and forward looking.

Like us all, as you moved through life you experienced hurt, resentment, grudges, fears and anger from the negativity directed by others to you. The sad part of all this is it is yourself you are harming if you hold on to these negative feelings.

> **The ability to forgive completely and generously is a hallmark of a truly healthy personality.**

The opposite of forgiveness is a tendency to hold grudges for long periods of time - for some even a lifetime. The inability to forgive and let bygones be bygones is the cause of many people carrying around with them negative feelings and bitterness held since unpleasant experiences that have occurred in their life.

The only way you can ever become free of these negative feelings and the harm they cause you is by learning to forgive readily. Learn to forgive all the time, so you never allow negative garbage to build up in your mind, this bitterness and anger, these grudges you tend to hang on to.

> **Forgiveness does not mean you condone what was done to you, or agree it was an acceptable thing to happen.**

It is never productive to deal with the past, present or future in an unforgiving way

As you consider the benefits of love and forgiveness, as opposed to hate, self-pity, anger, resentment and other negative emotions, you might like to consider that forgiveness is the easiest way to heal anything in your past that needs healing.

Forgiveness is not always **easy** of course. However forgiveness in this sense doesn't mean agreeing that the hurt that you experienced and caused you pain, was right. It is a more fundamental forgiveness. It means leaving the past in the past where it belongs.

If you find difficulty in doing this, it is well to realise that when you indulge in self-pity, resentment, anger and even hate, what you are actually doing is allowing the past to continue to harm and hurt you in the present. *Well isn't that so true?* If you still allow yourself to be a victim rather than an ingenious survivor of life, you are mucking up your life not anybody else's.

It is always better to recognise you are an ingenious survivor rather than a victim of circumstances. When you perceive yourself as a victim you tend to indulge in negative thinking about anything in the past that you feel was harmful and hurt you badly. The result is you continue to harm yourself more and more.

One of the greatest stories of self-belief in modern times must be the life of Nelson Mandela. Imprisoned for more than 27 years, living most of that time in a small cell, he never lost faith in his self-belief. This is why he was able to keep true to his beliefs and never lost faith in his dreams and aspirations for his country.

Nelson Mandela, when he was released from prison, was able to live a life of happiness, success and fulfilment through a supreme act of forgiveness that was founded in self-belief.

Shortly after his release from prison a reporter confronted him and said. "Mr Mandela you must really hate the people who kept you incarcerated for so long - you will surely never forgive them."

"No not at all," he replied. "I do not have any time for hate, anger, resentment or regret. I have the rest of my life to get on with and I am certainly not going to be shackled by the past. I forgive everybody and ask everybody to forgive me. Let us now live our lives positively and help create together what I have always believed in."

So he continued his life as a supremely happy person who the whole world loved, revered and respected and all because of his unerring belief in himself. This is a wonderful example of forgiveness. He left the past in the past where it belonged and got on with the future.

Later a reporter remarked. "Mr Mandela you showed such generosity of spirit when you were released from prison."

"Thank you," he replied, "but you must realise I said those words and had those feelings for my own wellbeing, not just for the good of my tormentors."

Above all, Nelson Mandela inspired those who have endured great hardship for many years, to have the self-belief that they can end up a winner.

As you consider the benefits of forgiveness, take a deep breath in and as you breathe out relax and drift to your special place where you feel safe, peaceful, tranquil, relaxed and in control.

The Self-Belief of Infancy

Consider now that ever since you were born you have learned many things but nothing more important than when you were an infant. Do you realise you were born with the powerful resources of self-belief to show determination, courage, confidence, motivation and the ability to continue carrying on until you achieved what you wanted to.

You may well ask *"How can that be?"* Well let me remind you how...

Remember as an infant when you noticed the carpet close up and the little interesting things on the carpet and were able to clearly see the underside of tables.

After a while you got tired of these limitations and tried to pull yourself up. You did this time and time again. You tried to sit up and you fell down. You pulled yourself up and did it again and again, again and again - hundreds of times until you could sit up.

Then you tried to crawl. You put one arm down and collapsed, then the other arm down and collapsed, then you tried to pull your legs forward and collapsed. You tried to do this hundreds of times until you learnt the motor skills of being able to crawl. You were using the resources you were born with: determination, courage, confidence and the self-belief to persevere until you achieved what you wanted.

You then stood up and experimented as to how you could start walking. Perhaps you held on to someone's hand or the side of a couch and you looked at the world differently from that time on. Rather than looking down, now you could look straight ahead and what you saw looked very different. You then started to run, talk and feed yourself and dress yourself, trying time and time again. So all these self-belief achievements changed the things you were interested in. They changed the way you reacted to your surroundings. Above all else they changed what you could do. It considerably widened your choices in life.

To achieve all these changes you used all the resources you were born with: determination to succeed and courage of your convictions. You did it using your 'I can do it' resources and belief in your ability to do what you wanted to do. You had the motivation to achieve and the ability to keep carrying on until you achieved what you wanted to achieve. You had the <u>self-belief</u> to do all these marvellous things you accomplished as an infant. So you must be convinced now. *Well aren't you?* If not keep going through these infant acts of self-belief until you are, because you may not realise or even know the skills and resources you already have within you.

Your childhood is evidence you can get in touch with your natural creativity and use imaginative ways to remind yourself about all you have already achieved. It is then a natural progression to get a new perspective on this or that situation, and allow new positive patterns to dominate your internal dialogue and thinking. A fresh, positive clarity spontaneously emerges, as you believe more and more in you.

The Power of Unconditional Love

Take the opportunity now to go back through the years and get in touch with all those marvellous things you did, all that sitting up, crawling, standing up and go back to that infant you and just imagine you are there.

You can say whatever you want to say. It's you you're talking to in absolute privacy, so you can be as heartfelt as you want to be.

Can you feel the love you have for the child that is you, the compassion you have, the undying faith and belief in that child? With that love is a quiet determination nothing is ever going to cause you lack of self-belief again.

You then become aware of an emerging sense of confidence when you practice these mind patterns repeatedly. You also realise that something you thought might have been awkward or embarrassing to do, turns out to be the most natural thing you could possibly do, once you realise the profound positive benefits you get from it.

Imagine how good you feel when you see that love as internal imagery of you, the adult holding the infant you and talking to yourself as an infant. Picture the love that pours through you to that child. It reminds me of when my old Nan put her loving arms around me and said. "Mike I love and believe in you," and as I loved and trusted my Nan, I believed her.

As the adult, feel inside and notice if you are giving yourself the same love you are giving that child. Being more and more curious about what you're going to learn, about what happens when you start to use these thoughts and feelings easily and effortlessly.

Have unconditional faith and belief in you.

Just imagine you are picking up yourself as an infant and give that little child a great big hug. This can bring a tear to the eye; certainly you can feel emotional because you often don't have an understanding of yourself. You can say to that wide-eyed innocent child "nothing is going to harm you, I am here for you, you are safe with me, I give you my unconditional love, I believe in you."

When you begin to get in touch with your own needs, then you'll start to allow the necessary changes you desire to take place in your life. As you accept yourself at a deep level, then you'll free yourself to change whatever you want to change. You become more influential in your life than you ever thought possible.

> **Feeling genuine self-liking and self-respect are nothing whatsoever to do with being arrogant, showing off, or telling everybody how marvellous you are, <u>not at all</u>. They are a quiet inner belief that allows you to feel worthwhile in your own eyes, comfortable within yourself and happy to be you.**

As you consider the benefits of all those positive feelings, move forward from that childhood experience and very comfortably let go of all those worries or resentments, {even possibly 'hate') of years gone by. All those little frightened voices, just let them go, they are not important any more. You do not give them any more power to cause lack of self- belief in your life ever again.

Now meet your new friend. There will be quiet development internally and as that happens it means you can make any changes about yourself you desire. You become aware of the many subtle ways in which you change. You know this because your belief and faith in yourself just grows and grows. You guide yourself to know and believe in you and you do just that, you do exactly that! One of the things you're really going to like about all this is how important your feeling of self-belief becomes and the feeling of power and control this gives you

Handling Negativity with Humour

When you are being too serious about your anxieties and fears it often serves you well to think about things in a humorous way. *Why not change the old doom-ridden way of tackling negative thinking? Why not use humour instead?*

When you choose to use humour more readily in dealing with unwanted emotions; you can feel lighter and lighter about them. You can use humour as another way to handle negative chatter and negative thinking. You can stand back and observe and listen to what a lot of old rubbish most of that negative inner dialogue really is.

You worry about so many things that don't happen anyway. All those negative 'what if' questions - very few of them ever come true. If this negative thinking happens maybe you'll say, "wait a minute, that is me going through all that old negative stuff again." So stop and observe it, even write it down sometimes, it can be so funny. Look at it in a humorous way, not in the limiting, lack of self-belief way.

We are all very funny people, *well aren't we?* We indulge compulsively in this useless negative mind chatter. Most of it is absolutely untrue, yet we believe what is going on in our head. Actually there is very little truth in it. You might already be thinking how great it would be to use humour in your life, to deal with all that negative thinking and in all sorts of humorous ways.

Remember when you can laugh at most of those things that previously caused you grief, you have arrived at the point where positive self-development can progress. You know at that point you are on the right track. It's good to feel your self-belief growing day by day. *That's wonderful, isn't it?*

Bring as much humour as possible to every situation, where humour is permissible.

How would it be if you stopped worrying and started living? How will you feel when you do that?

The sooner you just let go and accept that in many cases life is just life, sometimes good, sometimes difficult or even hurtful, the sooner you will realise negative mind chatter nags away at your self-belief and you will realise there isn't any merit in engaging in it. Know it holds no value for you and just say "I refuse to give this negativity any more power in my life"

A Clearer Path Ahead

Just treat that crazy talk not with fear as a demon but just as monkey chatter. Say "No that is not for me. I don't want that anymore, that's not a reflection of who I am. I don't go down that old pathway now." You don't have to believe the negative chatter. It may be there, to some extent, but you don't have to let it limit your ambition in life. You now have many options open to you to deal with all that negative stuff, which previously weakened your self-belief. You will have many opportunities to make choices on the positive pathway you are now travelling along.

In your daily life change your way of thinking. Cancel out and change…

- "I am frightened to do it" into "I am full of courage."
- "I can't!" Into "I can."
- "I can't change" into "I can and I will change."

If you keep using the "I can and I will" self-belief system - something positive happens

Using Experiences Positively

You might want, instead of that old negative thinking, to do the following. Go back to a time in your life when you did something really well, when you did something good for yourself or somebody else. Start focusing on those things. Think of a good thought you had a beautiful thing you have seen or a wonderful experience you have shared. Think of the love you have given to others, your mother, your father, a friend, a lover or a pet, anyone and anything - it matters not whom or what. Be aware of the good things you have enjoyed on your own. Stack up those good memories and let them dwell in your mind and banish that old unwanted redundant negative thinking.

So you have been examining your self-belief and have read many suggestions that you can use to strengthen it. Think of all the times you could have been defeated by a situation but carried on and won through. Just look at how you have risen above so much and how you have met many challenges. Look at the courage it took to be where you are in your life now.

Living In the Present – Not The Past

Why not look at your good points, your virtues? Look at what you have created from the time you were born until now. Why not focus on all that is good in your life. So you shift your perceptions all the time from negative to positive, moving away from any guilt, any shame or any judgement of others or yourself.

It does not matter how you forgive. The benefit comes from your doing it. Think of how amazing you will feel knowing you have done all these positive things for yourself, as you move towards the new you and realise all the possibilities that go with it.

So I really want to take this opportunity to congratulate you. You have begun to succeed in the search for emotional contentment. You are firmly on the pathway to success. You have made a commitment to yourself. Now you have the choice of living your life the way you want to. *Wouldn't you agree that to have a much stronger belief in yourself, than you could have ever imagined possible, would be fantastic? How good does that make you feel?*

The Observing Self – Using the Past Positively

You can be the 'observing self' of what has happened in your life and what you can achieve in the future, by detaching yourself from all the usual complexities of everyday life. This is one of the most effective ways to turn the changes you want to make into effective outcomes.

When you use imagination as the observing self, to look over the significant events of your life, you can use the feedback you receive to guide your future actions with clear perspective and purpose. You can look upon your life and the path you have taken, right up to the present moment, in new and constructive ways. The further you stand back from something the clearer you see the whole picture.

You realise failures are the best learning experiences you can have. As you become the observer of your journey, you can also re-live those times of positive achievement. You use this opportunity to celebrate positive progress and learn new and empowering information.

With your powers of imagination you can explore the past, present and the future. Your imagination and feelings allow you to see the future, as you want it to be. You can anticipate events, plan your next move and implement new behaviours with self-belief and conviction. When you do something new, your imagination and feelings help you proceed courageously, knowing you can minimise the risks and maximise the return with every decision you make.

The experience you need for success comes from interacting with life, taking action and observing the effect. Each time you observe the effect of your actions your self-belief drives you forward. You recognise what you really want to do and take the next step forward decisively. You know your innate resources are fully available to you as a guide for future positive progress.

Your beliefs provide the cornerstone of all your thinking. They determine your inner dialogue whether it is negative or positive. Your thoughts create your feelings, which then colour your decisions. That in turn affect the choices you make. If you keep reinforcing your negative beliefs with consistent negative inner dialogue you create negative self-fulfilling prophecies. From this it is clear to see how important it is to form your beliefs on actual reality and not on what you believe is reality. "I feel inferior. I feel worthless. I am unlucky, everything I do goes wrong" and other such nominal beliefs are not true facts but emotional statements.

With self-belief you are truly empowered, as sure as the tide flows in and out. Positive self-belief guides you ever forward no matter where your life may lead you.

With belief the seemingly impossible can be made possible. In 1954 Dr Roger Bannister (later Sir Roger Bannister) became the first man ever to run a mile in less than four minutes. This was something that had previously been believed to be impossible. Yet Dr Bannister's success proved that it could be done – and swept away the belief it was impossible to achieve. For thousands of years, no athlete had ever run the four-minute mile as far as anybody knew. Yet within one year of Bannister's achievement, more than one hundred athletes around the world ran a mile in less than four minutes. It wasn't because their bodies had suddenly changed to become stronger or faster. It was because their beliefs about what was possible had been transformed – and their bodies responded to **those beliefs**.

> **The body performs. The mind achieves.**

Subconscious Mind Exercise (One)

Make sure you are in a safe, relaxed, comfortable situation so your focus is on what you are doing and nothing else needs your attention.

Read through the relaxation process in chapter 4 pages 37-40. You will now be familiar with it, having used the relaxation exercise before.

Read through the section headed 'The power of unconditional love' earlier in this chapter and become very familiar with it. Then close your eyes. Take several deep breaths in and out and as you let each breath out say to yourself, "I relax deep inside". Go through the relaxation process, then work with that infant which was you, as you go through the process outlined in 'the power of unconditional love.' Do this for 10 minutes or more and then repeat it often thereafter, and just witness what a <u>difference</u> this makes to how you feel about you.

Subconscious Mind Exercise (Two)

Once again make sure you are in a safe, comfortable situation so your focus is on what you are doing and nothing else needs your attention.

Read through the section on 'The observing self' earlier in this chapter and become very familiar with it. Then carry out the 'closed eyes relaxation' and go through the process of working with the 'observing self'. Do this a number of times.

With belief in you, create in your mind and in your imagination a successful future, one that meets your needs, aspirations and dreams. Imagine yourself breaking out of your safety zones and get beyond your limiting beliefs. Do this frequently. It is a very powerful process.

NB. *Please remember* - Because of the relaxation element in the subconscious mind exercises, they should <u>never</u> be done when you need to be alert.

CHAIN, ROPE STRING AND AN ELEPHANT

So you want a life of success, happiness and fulfilment and more control of your life, your emotions, feelings and behaviour. You want to make positive changes and have greater <u>self-belief</u>.

If you say to me, "I have tried but I can't seem to believe in myself, well not fully in the way I really want to. I still feel I'm on a leash, I can't feel really free to live how I want;" then I am reminded of the story of the elephant that when young, was tied to a large post by a length of strong chain.

As much as the elephant tried it could not break the chain and free itself so that it could grow up and develop fully in the way it wanted, like so many other elephants do.

So it grew up to believe it couldn't develop. It felt restricted, enclosed, confined. When it tried to pull hard to free itself, it did not do so with real conviction and sometimes it really hurt. The elephant wanted so much to be free, happy and confident, to feel good and do all it wanted to do but felt it was never in a position to do that. It so much wanted to change and develop in a much freer and more flexible way and to live a successful and happy life.

So as the elephant grew up, it continued to believe it did not have the strength to free itself. In reality the metal chain had at some time been changed into a rope and it could easily break the rope with the strength it had developed growing up through years of toil and endeavour and set itself free.

However, because the elephant believed it couldn't do so, it continued its life with this belief.

In fact the rope - far from becoming stronger and stronger became weaker and weaker. It had over time been changed from a rope to just a very light tether of string, but because in the elephant's mind it was still a metal chain, and because it had tried so often to change and break free, it continued to believe it just wasn't possible. As it believed, so it was.

The self-belief that the elephant could free itself just wasn't there - for the perception it allowed to dwell persistently in its mind, it manifested into its life. It became a self-fulfilling prophecy.

One day the elephant was taken out into the wild open country that tantalising always surrounded it. The elephant was only tied to a tree with a very flimsy piece of string. After a while, an elephant from the wild open country seeing the tethered elephant tried to encourage it to follow him out into the freedom beyond. The elephant was taken many times to the edge of the free land beyond and although it had been encouraged by the free elephant to follow him, it did not do so because it believed it was tethered to the tree by a thick metal chain.

After sometime, early one morning, a new horizon, a new beginning, the dawn of a new day, the tethered elephant gazed out into the free land beyond. On the horizon he could see the most glorious crimson sky with golden streaks running through it.

There before the elephant was this absolutely marvellous awe-inspiring sight. Suddenly the tethered elephant felt a great surge of freedom from within. "I must reach that beautiful sight beyond. I must be there." It surged forward not thinking about the 'mental tether' that had always held it back in the past. The flimsy string broke so easily that the elephant wondered why it had allowed itself to be restricted for so long. It could really sense it was now able to move towards a life of much greater freedom, happiness, success and fulfilment

The elephant realised what it thought it couldn't do turned out, in fact, to be the most natural thing in the world to do. We can easily see that when we really know. Whatever has been tied into a knot can be untied and whatever mental knots that have been tied up by the mind can be untied by the mind and set free. If the knots are very tight it can take a little time but certainly it can be done. Therefore 'knots' can become 'can do's' if we make them things we <u>really believe</u> we can achieve, not just wishes, tries, hopes, or dreams. Imagine how your life will be when you achieve all that freedom.

CHAPTER NINE: SHARING IN THE ABUNDANCE OF LIFE

The abundance of life is not only for the favoured few. It is available for us all. However it will only become available to you if you recognise it is your right to have 'abundance.' Be courageous and gather sufficient 'abundance' for your needs. Read through the 'Mental Law of Control' again, on pages 49-51, then continue reading this chapter, which develops the idea of abundance and what it really means.

Many people are deterred from obtaining what they want to achieve by underrating themselves and comparing themselves unfavourably with other people. Do your best and be 'you.' In that way you will be successful and obtain abundance in a way that is right for you.

Asking the Right Questions

To move towards the abundance you desire, why not ask yourself these questions:

A variety of self-limiting questions can go through your mind. Maybe you simply haven't opened up to the unlimited possibilities around and within you.

How would you react if you asked yourself these questions?

- "Have I all the happiness, peace, joy and success I want?
- *Am I living my life to my full potential?*
- *If I had a fulfilled life, would I be a better person to know?"*

The Choice is Always Yours

Surely the answer is, "Why not, you deserve abundance just as much as anyone else does. It is up to you to achieve it. The choice is yours.

Maybe you haven't thought of all the ways you can enjoy abundance. So why not decide what you want that will bring a better quality of life to you as an individual and unique person. Then effectively use your mind to help you tap into the abundance all around you. Do it now. Ask yourself:

"How can I achieve the abundance in my life that I am searching for, to experience joy with family life, joy in my surroundings, joy with my outlook on life and a powerful feeling of well-being?"

Why not consider thinking in this way:

"I would like the abundance that comes from a greater peace by not listening to external or internal negative voices of criticism. I believe in the abundance of unconditional self-respect, self-worth and self-liking from me to me. I would like unnecessary doubt removed so I can fully function in my world of joy and contentment. I seek the abundance of peace that will give me the sense of who I am and where I want to be and what is best for a successful life for me."

> **Bring abundance into your life in a way that best suits you.**

Imagine yourself for a moment observing children playing in a park, or on a beach, or after it has snowed. Just hear the laughter and the fun. Listen to the joy that lack of fear brings. Witness the joy that the abundance of life brings. You will then realise how much your peace, your joy, your happiness means to you as an adult. *How does that feel?*

You may of course change the abundance you desire from time to time and alter your abundance goals. Because times change, people change and situations change. Always in your awareness you are drawn to that which is in your best interest and in the best interest of those you love. Fully focus on the changes you want to make to enrich your life. That doesn't mean hoping or dreaming but really believing and achieving.

You have read a lot in this book about negative mind chatter and the benefits you obtain by changing it into positive inner dialogue. One way that has already been mentioned in this book is the use of positive internal imagery, often called visualisation. Imprint on your mind the abundance you desire, seeing yourself in your mind enacting and receiving the abundance you want.

> **You can achieve the abundance in your life you desire.**

You have to keep doing this frequently, (remember the subconscious mind works by programming). It must be exposed to this positive inner dialogue and positive inner mind imagery frequently and the more frequently you do this, the more effective it is.

Just think how frequently you have engaged in the negative stuff and how ineffective that has been. In the days and weeks ahead you begin to notice certain indications that what you desire is happening as you become more and more interested in making abundance an irresistible influence in your life. You can do that by realising that although material abundance costs money, the most important aspects of abundance are freely available.

The past has gone. Save your mind energy for the abundance of the future. Does the past represent *the life you want?* If not, change is the only meaningful way forward. Realise how valuable every second of your life is. Going over any perceived lack of abundance in the past is a total waste of your time. It achieves nothing positive in your life now.

Choice is power and gives you control. Do you use the phrase "I had no choice, I had to do it"? This in reality is never true because you always have a choice to do one thing or the other. What you actually imply when you say, "I had no choice," is that you are claiming the choice wasn't your responsibility because you had to do it. The "I always have a choice" statement is not easy to accept, but if you really think about it, choosing to do or not to do something as an adult, however you view it, is always your choice.

The choice now is that you can turn to the old life and say:

"This is what I know, I have never had very much and never will, and therefore that's how my life is and always will be."

Alternatively you can turn to a new future and say.

"I know there is abundance in the world I live in and I choose to share in it."

Remember you do have a choice. You always have a choice, however difficult some choices may be. Not making choices and the 'old chestnut' "I don't have a choice" are some of the greatest causes of stress, worry and fear in the human mind.

Make your choice saying:

"I choose to be amongst the deserving. I choose to be calm, relaxed and confident. I choose to allow myself to cope with fear and stress and above all to be who I am. I choose to be me."

You can then wonder what it would be like for you to take a fresh look at this life of yours and wonder how quickly you'll begin to notice the abundance that you desire becoming a part of your daily life.

> **Always keep in mind it is not people, situations or experiences that cause us anxiety, stress and fear but our perceptions of them.**

Within this knowledge and understanding is the secret of a life of happiness, success and abundance, as opposed to a life in a straitjacket of anxiety, fear and stress.

If you continue to struggle with your right to abundance, ask your subconscious mind to bring the clarity and guidance that would be useful in letting go of that negative thinking.

You can stop the thoughts that suggest "I am not deserving. "If you do not, your struggle will continue until you decide you don't want all that old negative thinking. You can now resolve any doubt you may have by knowing every time any fear issue arises you resolve it. Think how you will rejoice when in your darkest feelings, in the most confusing place you can be your positive resources are always available for you to use.

See through the illusion, fear and pain of the moment. Set your desires for abundance in your life and have an awareness that no matter what happens, abundance can be yours. Then you can obtain it. All it takes is persistence of purpose, carrying on, carrying on until you have achieved the abundance you desire.

Believing In You

When you start to believe in you, success will happen much more quickly than you could have ever imagined. You become aware of a new range of possibilities when you allow your subconscious mind to start generating solutions. You become aware of a growing confidence in yourself as you practise thinking in this new abundant way. Things begin to move away from 'very unlikely' to 'it's possible'. When you are in the middle of something that isn't working, simply switch over to knowing that there is abundance. It isn't an illusion. It is a reality.

There is endless abundance all around you and nobody is separated from it, unless you make personal choices, which prevent you enjoying this abundance. If you do not separate yourself from abundance but accept you are indeed a part of it, you can receive it. You then see a new direction opening up in front of you and will enhance this positive thinking, even as you sleep and dream. So don't listen to those who say 'you must be humble and feel undeserving,' that is their problem, not yours. If you have some religious doubts about this, remember it was said, 'ask and it will be given unto you.'

Open up your mind and allow that abundance to be there. When you are positive about abundance, observe and see how changes happen. You will be aware of a sense of real enjoyment as you continue to practice these positive mind patterns every day of your life. Seek your share of abundance. Generate the mental energy that helps you towards what you want to achieve.

Handling Fear

Have a sense that everything is all right; it will all work out well. If there are doubts, if "I don't deserve" comes back, just look back into the past. Is there something you have still not dealt with? *Is there something you are still hiding that you still gloss over, a lingering fear perhaps? Is there a doubt of some kind? Is there a perception you still need to work on and adjust?* I'm not suggesting you will find something, just that you can learn in many different ways, at many different times and in many different situations and the fact you do learn means you can gain the knowledge you need to overcome any doubts or fears.

Now feel for a moment what it's like without unnecessary fear - because that can be a little unnerving, a little frightening. It can seem somewhat unnatural, not to be worrying and anxious. Thinking irrationally becomes so familiar. You can seem lost without it. So what are you going to put in place of that old unnecessary fear?

So continue your journey as you move away from the negative side into your special place, a place of hope and belief for the future. Allow yourself the confidence to receive the abundance you want. Let it grow and grow. When you really begin to get in touch with your own needs then you'll start to allow the necessary changes towards abundance to take place in your life. So put that new found goal for abundance securely into your safe place, deep inside and leave it there forever.

When you accept yourself as you are then you'll free yourself to change whatever you want to. You are probably already aware it is so easy to let go of all that old baggage from the past. It's easy to move past the unnecessary fear because you now have the mind tools to do it. Make these positive thoughts as regular as breathing in and out. You then become more influential than you ever thought possible in guiding your life forward positively, in an abundant way.

You may, of course, feel that negative thinking again from time to time. It could be words drifting to you from the past from parents, from a teacher, from anyone in your former years saying to you in your head:

'Why do you think you are deserving of anything?"
You will never attain what you are looking for."

Just listen to those negative thought patterns for a moment. Ask yourself:

"What mind exercise can I use to let that go?

As you start thinking in this positive way about abundance you'll enjoy a real sense of achievement and you'll allow your subconscious mind to generate creative solutions, which suit your own particular unique needs and aspirations. Notice how more positive you feel when:

You no longer take part in negative thinking. You no longer believe it. In due time the negative thinking will surely enter less and less into your mind because of your more dominant positive self-talk. You can imagine yourself enjoying the benefits of having made all the changes about yourself you desired. Notice what happens when you imagine being able to do all these things effortlessly and easily.

As you go through the process of change, your life will be much happier. Observe what you desire both personally and in your connection with the world around you. Watch it just grow and grow in a positive way. What a wonderful feeling that is. One of the things you're really going to love about your self-development is noticing all the changes you want to make about yourself appearing in your life as easily as your name does, go ahead imagine all you want **happening now!**

Working Effectively With Your Subconscious Mind.

Make sure you are in a safe, relaxed, comfortable situation so your focus is on what you are doing and nothing else needs your attention. Read the following a few times until you are familiar with its content:

Have a look at any aspect of fear based on lack of abundance in your life. It could be something you have buried inside yourself. Focus your awareness on it. You may be aware of that old "You can't have it, don't be silly and be happy with the little you have." Or you may be uncertain where that fear comes from. Say to yourself:

"Wherever it comes from, I don't care because I am not going to give it any more power."

If you deny anything its energy and power it cannot operate it cannot exist any longer.

> **Refuse to give irrational fear any more power. It is no longer a part of who you are.**

If that fear continues, that doubt persists, be persistent yourself and keep going through the subconscious mind exercise below until any fear just falls away from you, its power completely gone.

However make sure the abundance you seek is really what you want. You do not need abundance of everything, only an abundance of that which brings genuine happiness into your life.

> **Always be aware of the abundance you genuinely need.**

> **Subconscious Mind Exercise**
>
> Now go through the relaxation shown in chapter 4, pages 37-40. Then think about any aspect of abundance you desire in your life. Work for ten minutes or so or longer if you have time. Persistence of purpose is important.
>
>   Keep carrying out this subconscious mind work until all the abundance issues have been resolved. Then visualise your future with all the abundance you desire already achieved. All the time engage in 'can do thoughts' visualising yourself as a person with the strength to take action see your thoughts becoming reality in this wonderful abundant world.
>
>   If you tap into this abundance you will <u>achieve what you want. Change what you think and you change how you live.</u>

NB. *Please remember* - Because of the relaxation element in the subconscious mind exercises, they should <u>never</u> be done when you need to stay alert for some reason.

The Sunflower.

A sunflower seed blew into a dark and dank wood and there tried to develop and grow. As it started to struggle up it did so with great effort and difficulty. It did grow to some extent because the drive for survival is present in every living thing. However the sunflower found life a great struggle. Its stem was somewhat thin and weak, its leaves small and pallid and its flower head a rather insipid yellow and very small.

This struggle went on for some time and the sunflower seemed to have almost given up the fight to believe there was enough abundance in the wood for all the trees, plants and creatures to flourish.

One day a fierce storm blew and knocked down some of the trees that had been excluding the direct sunlight from reaching the sunflower. It could now be clearly seen there was abundance for growth shining down onto the wood; it had only been obscured from view.

However the sunflower was still very confused because it had been used to the darkness and what it perceived as lack of light. Each day it turned away from the sun towards the shade and darkness because this is the way it had created by its habitual behaviour and did not react to the actual territory it lived in.

It moved towards the shade and darkness, away from the abundance of light and energy. "This is what I'm used to and familiar with, better the devil you know" the sunflower thought. It didn't realise the darkness it was facing moved it away from the abundance that surrounded it and therefore it allowed the darkness to make it weaker and weaker.

The sunflower continued to be confused and each day, instead of moving its diminutive flower head towards the sun, it moved away from it. Each day the sunflower moved in the direction of least benefit to it still believing there was insufficient abundance of light to realise its full growth and potential. This went on for what seemed like an eternity to the sunflower.

The sunflower continued to believe not enough sunshine was available to nourish it and help it grow strong and flourish as it wanted to. So it continued moving away from the light towards the darkness in the old habitual way, away from the abundance that was available for every plant in the wood.

One day some sunflower seeds were blown near to the struggling sunflower. They used the abundance surrounding them to flourish. These seeds grew vigorously and quickly and very soon developed long thick strong stems with large round flower heads and a beautiful golden rich yellow flower the size of a dinner plate.

The depleted and weary sunflower watched the other sunflowers grow quickly and strongly. After studying them for quite a while the diminutive sunflower noticed what the healthy ones were doing. It noticed every morning as soon as the sun came up they started turning their flower heads towards the abundance of the sun's golden rays

Each and every day they went through the same process of turning their heads always towards the sun. Even more interesting, the struggling sunflower noticed that even if it was cloudy, raining or stormy the sunflowers still moved around all day, always towards the sun. It realised the most important truth of all, that even when it's cloudy, however black the clouds are or however heavy the rain or strong the storm is, the sun still shines in all its glory above the darkness and lower down, warming every living thing. Its abundance never failed to be available, sometimes weak, sometimes average, and sometimes very strong but it was always there.

At last the confused sunflower realised what was most beneficial for it to grow and develop its full potential. Each morning it always turned itself towards the sun even if the sky above was cloudy and dark. It followed the sun each and every day

Surely and safely the deprived sunflower grew taller and stronger. Its leaves grew wider and greener and its flower turned from a pallid yellow into the vibrant yellow of sunshine. It continued in this way until it had achieved the success every living thing can achieve. It realised abundance is there for all to obtain.

CHAPTER TEN: THE CONFIDENCE TO BE YOU

*As a child, or even later in your teenage years, did you often feel there were conditions you had to adhere to in order to receive the **love** every child needs?*

As a child you naturally looked for approval from people around you, in particular those from whom you most desired unconditional love. If you feel this was not freely given it could have caused feelings of emotional abandonment. It can then lead to feelings of not being loved for who you are. If childhood experiences seem to be repeated in later life, the earlier hurtful feelings can be enhanced. You could still be striving for unconditional love.

You are the only person who can truly validate you and release any feelings of emotional abandonment. As an adult you have a great deal more realisation about who you are, than you did as a child. If as an adult, you depend on validation from anybody else as to what you say and do, you are giving away your power to others. You are saying I cannot feel good about myself unless others give me permission to do so.

You have learnt a great deal from the previous chapters in this book and used your subconscious mind to work on the important personal changes you want to make. Now it is time to face the most profound aspects of yourself so you can complete your 'journey of discovery.' The most important part of you, indeed of anybody: the confidence to be you. This is when you realise at a profound level of consciousness that what you think about yourself as a person actually dictates almost every thought you have, including your actions, beliefs and behaviour. This realisation can be an irresistible springboard for positive change.

A powerful way of assessing your self-esteem is to ask yourself these questions:
- *"Do I take the best care of me that I possibly can?*
- *Do I like me?*
- *Have I genuine feelings of self-respect, self-liking and self-worth for me?*
- *Am I my own best friend?"*

Many people are still brought up with the idea they should be humble because feeling good about oneself is somehow bad. In this chapter you will be using your mind in powerful ways. This will help you explore your innermost self and give you a real sense of empowerment and what you can do with the knowledge you gain about yourself. As you go through this thought provoking process you can obtain great benefit from it. This part of your journey is a very defining one, if you allow it to be.

I suggest you now take yourself to that special place that lies deep within, the place of warmth, comfort, security, relaxation, tranquillity, peace and control, the place that is the real you, a place of nurturing and change.

Now you are going to meet a new friend, and while you do this, nothing can hurt you or harm you in any way whatsoever. It is all to do with learning about you. Some people have told you about this friend and how much the friend is liked by them. They accept you as an 'okay' person. You have a lot to discover about this new friend. I would like to suggest you feel an excitement about this, even if you have to go back some way and rekindle childlike enthusiasm and trust, to enjoy meeting the real you.

Just go to that childhood time, now! Find the excitement that was there. Remember what it was like to do something new, something different! Really feel love for yourself as a child. Then give that love to the adult you, the same love that you are giving to that little child.

> **You have done your best in life and that is all anyone can do at anytime and in any circumstances.**

The Mirror of Self

The self-examination you undertake in the 'mirror of self' process isn't easy. It is a real challenge because it goes to the very core of whom and what you are. It has to be repeated and experienced many times to get the full value and benefit from it. However when you do, it will change you in a way little else ever can. Your self-esteem, your feelings of self-worth and self-respect will soar tremendously and then you can really continue your life as your own best friend.

The love it is suggested you express in 'the mirror of self' is not showing off, it is not bragging or being conceited or the "here everybody what a wonderful person I am" way of expressing yourself. It is a deep profound unconditional love for you. Said by you to you; it does not concern anybody else. You say it to yourself in private. It is about genuine feelings of self-respect and self-worth. You don't have to show off or brag about yourself to show you have genuine self-esteem. People with genuine self-esteem show it to others in many subtle ways, in wholly natural ways, quietly and unobtrusively, in unassuming ways.

Sit quietly and focus on that inner safety, security, peace, tranquillity and relaxation of your special place.

Ask yourself these questions:

- *Do you know the essence of you?*
- *Do you respect and like the person you are?*

If not, if there is doubt, I suggest you pause for a second and ask yourself this question:

"How can I improve the quality of my life? What changes do I still have to make about the person I want to be?"

> **It is only by asking frank and honest questions that you can seek the answers you need.**

So why not allow yourself to be very peaceful again because you may well find that you are feeling slightly upset or uncertain, or even a little fearful and you could find yourself being critical as well. Just listen to that mind chatter. *What are you thinking now?* Now, work out how you can let any negative critical, doubting chatter go. Just release it. Choose your own way; you have already practised effective ways of doing this. Release any guilt or doubt surrounding self-esteem issues. Just let them go, release them, leave them in the past where they belong.

When detached from your inner wisdom, your mind can lead you a merry dance and can convince you of all sorts of falsehoods. There can still be some distorted stories from the past that create fears and misguided perceptions.

It is important to look beyond your superficial self. Disregard how you look and the shape of your body. Bypass your entire external appearance. Look beyond the 'packaging' that surrounds you. Turn off the mental chatter in your head. Go deep into your inner self. You cannot change your external appearance in any basic way. You can, however, change distorted thinking and negative behaviour and how you live your life and how you use your mind. These things you can definitely change.

As you focus deep within, say to yourself. *"I don't know you as much as I would like to, therefore I am going to take the time to find out <u>everything</u> about you, emotions and all. <u>When I do,</u> I will honestly be able to say, I am happy to be me."*

This is a profound way to achieve the emotional confidence you have always desired.

Now that you have met yourself in this very intimate way, you realise there are a whole new set of opportunities and possibilities that arise from this because you have been operating frequently, often with separate parts of you fighting with each other.

Why not make up your mind to take very good care of yourself. One of the things that can happen at some point is that you often become aware of your negative mind chatter about lack of confidence again - after all you are only human. For all your belief, for all your convictions, it can start up again. Now you have those mental coping processes in place, you just say "enough is enough." Watch and see how negative thoughts simply fade away. You don't have to work so persistently at letting go; you don't have to go through all the processes now because you know that negativity is no longer a dominant part of your more positive consciousness. You are now in the realm of real choice.

Now that you have this new friend, whatever further changes you want to make, carry them out with belief. Above all show the utmost respect for this best friend of yours. Just think of the new possibilities. Have the confidence to be you.

Much of the time you are involved with this process and reviewing it in your conscious awareness, there can be some doubt deep inside you that might still be saying, "I am still not certain about this. *How do I make sure this is all going to work?"* Belief is not always easy. Believing and trusting your emotional self can be hard in the beginning. It is, however, advantageous to imagine you already have genuine self-trust and just let your own naturalness come through. With your new friend, there aren't any dark corners that cannot be explored; there is just you, your friend and the abundance of the world you live in. As you accept this, why not look towards a better future, your future.

Find out who you really are. Having the confidence to be who you are, you will find that as you get to know yourself more, you experience less anxiety and stress. You will then have fewer and fewer thoughts of have to, need to, must do, ought to do and should do.

Use the powerful statement 'I want to and I am going to.'

Anxiety and fear are replaced with possibility. Problems are replaced by challenges. So you shift from the old way of living, to your new way of living. The new you can use humour as a coping strategy- humour you hardly ever used when you were busy being that previous more serious person worrying about life's difficulties. So the new person that you are becoming is the real you. You are giving a gift from you to you. You are moving steadily to becoming the natural you and using this new belief in your daily life. Now you begin to realise you have resources that you did not believe you had or forgot you had. Knowing this new person is all about possibilities, not restrictions. Indeed, you may have already become aware of so much that hasn't been possible in the past but that can be in the future.

You are on a journey of renewal. There is no room for the old demons here or self-punishment, negative self-criticism or recriminations. On the contrary you are going in a new positive direction. It is still possible to have some ambivalent feelings come to the fore. If they remain hidden you cannot deal with them.

Your pathway forward now is to deal with any remaining negative baggage that attempts to sabotage you. Say to yourself. "I will never allow that mental garbage into my life again," and really mean it. When you do that you can be confident about all the benefits it will bring.

If you now move towards discovery and progress rather than keeping the old outdated ways of thinking, you can change. There is now room in your mind to do so. The old negative way of thinking has been removed, thrown away like the old baggage it is. Any new negativity can be released from your life immediately, as it occurs. You cannot be absolutely free from negative thinking (nobody is perfect) but what you can do is prevent it settling and festering in your mind (it can do that if you are not on guard whenever it comes).

> **Show yourself compassion, instead of giving yourself a hard time. Tune your mind into all that is good about you and the world you live in.**

I read a biography of the singer and songwriter John Denver and somewhere in his book he wrote about the fact that his life changed when he realised he actually felt part of everything that he saw, heard, sung and wrote songs about. He was part of the air he breathed, the mountains, the oceans, the fields and the universe beyond. He and the water were the same. Everything flowed through him and he flowed through everything and if that is so, in his mind, everything was a part of him and him of it. And that is scientifically true. Everything that exists in the universe including our own planet and everything on it, originated from stardust. Wouldn't you agree how much better to believe you have this intimate connection with the wonder of the universe and the world you live in, rather than feeling you are separated from them?

Now take a moment to review what you have learned about doing this 'Mirror of Self' process: *Do you feel empowered?*

The process needs to be repeated until positive feelings of self-esteem are more dominant than the old negative feelings, until you are completely at ease with who you are. You can't make a mistake with this process. Just believe in you, so that each time you repeat your positive statements about self-esteem you give yourself permission to be your true self.

You have literally started a chain reaction for your whole life and although you may feel you have difficulty with coping because you're not achieving what you want to quickly enough, keep repeating the process and very soon - sooner than you may have ever imagined - you will have the confidence to be you - your own best friend.

> **Subconscious Mind Exercise**
>
> Place yourself in a safe, relaxed situation so you can focus on what you are doing and nothing else needs your attention.
>
> Make sure you are very familiar with the 'mirror of self' process explained earlier in this chapter then go through the relaxation exercise shown in chapter 4, pages 37-40.
>
> With your eyes closed, visualise going through the 'mirror of self' process.
>
> Make the following three statements:
> 1. "I am totally independent of the good or bad opinions of others
> 2. I am beneath no one and above no one;
> 3. I am fearless in the face of any and all challenges."

NB. *Please remember* – **Because of the relaxation element in subconscious mind exercises, they should <u>never</u> be done when** *you need to stay alert for some reason.*

This is a very powerful process, much more empowering than you might imagine. Like all the subconscious mind exercises, persistence of purpose provides results.

Isn't it just great to know you can be your best friend and how quickly you can make that true? One thing you'll really love about this is how it can be a real revelation. When you next open your eyes, you can be as relaxed about yourself as when your eyes are closed.

Mind Software

Like most people you probably know how to use a computer, they are now part of most people's lives.

However it doesn't matter in the least if you are not using correct computer procedures when using your mind software because your mind is far more flexible than a computer could ever be.

So create an imaginative system of your own, using the most powerful processes you can create. Your conscious mind doesn't even need to understand the logic of what you are doing but your subconscious mind certainly will. Your subconscious mind is very much like a computer but far more creative and more powerful than a machine could ever be.

Your subconscious mind stores all the events in your life and all your experiences, much like a computer database. It then translates these events and experiences into beliefs, feelings and behaviour.

However you know that sometimes computer anti-virus systems don't work and there can be various reasons for this. In most cases you don't know why it hasn't worked, just that it, doesn't. Sometimes computers don't work as you want them to and that is so frustrating.

Fortunately your brain is far more powerful than any computer could ever be. Much of it, in fact nearly all of it, works well. But certain parts affected by the equivalent of the computer virus or other malfunction can be troublesome.

So like the computer you have built your life up according to the things that have been programmed into your mind by the experiences you have had during your life. Of course many of the things you have programmed into your mind over the years have been and still are supportive and helpful. However sometimes they can be unhelpful and even downright troublesome in a very annoying and frustrating way.

You can have 'mind software programmes' that lead to low feelings of self-esteem. However just as you can use a computer mouse to create things and make changes in a computer using new software when appropriate, so you can with your brain. Now you can work on those negative programmes in your mind, likening it to a computer, dealing with doubts about self-esteem, self-liking and self-respect that prevent you from having the confidence to be you.

So now with your mind computer just like a desk - or laptop computer you can click on all programmes. Do that now and bring up all the negative programmes that are active in your life, affecting your self-esteem. Highlight one particular one. Take it right back to when it was first created.

So now you have highlighted the negative mind programme that has been causing you most self-esteem doubts. Surely it feels good that you now realise you are dealing with it in such a practical way. *Well doesn't it?* So now if you want to get rid of it, click delete. Unfortunately computer viruses can be obstinate and likewise programmed brain negativities can be.

Sometimes they can slip into the recycle bin of your brain, which means they are still lurking there and some little trigger can set them off again. You need to be persistent with this process to ensure negative thinking is also deleted from the recycle bin. If it ever pops up again, in some way or another, you can use a super delete and then click the 'okay' box to confirm it's completely eradicated. It is finally gone forever. You will know when this happens because you feel calmer and lighter as if a weight has been lifted from your shoulders. You experience a triumphant feeling. Whether that feeling happens consciously or subconsciously, it does not matter.

You can also create new positive programmes about how you want to be, how you want to behave, how you want to feel. Never form new programmes in the negative, (making them about how you don't want to feel, act or behave,) only how *you* want to be. Now create these new programmes using your mind and imagination in a new and creative way, so it all works for you automatically. Make sure each programme is exactly how you want it to be in every detail.

When you are sure each programme is completed give it a name, click the save button and create a programme folder for it in your mind data base system. This new programme will help you feel more confident, more competent, happier and healthier, both in mind and body and you will be able to use each new mind programme when and wherever you want by just taking a deep breath and saying to yourself the folder name. Then it can start working for you automatically.

So you are more and more in control of your thoughts, feelings, emotions and behaviour. Because of that, your actions are more positive, stronger and more powerful in respect of your self-esteem. Positive feelings of self-esteem flow all through your mind and body. You feel more and more confident, much more in control of your thoughts, actions and behaviour.

As you delete the negative programmes and replace them with positive ones, you realise negative mind viruses regarding self-esteem are much like computer viruses. They can be programmed in not knowing when and how it happened. However your subconscious mind, now you have shown it how, can highlight all negative self-esteem programmes, delete them and replace them with powerful positive programmes.

If in the future something in your life triggers a negative self-esteem thought that persists, you just take a deep breath in and out and say "delete" quietly but firmly with belief and conviction. Your life then becomes more and more under your control and you soon become calm and confident, knowing all is well with you.

You can, if you want to, make a mind software programme for more happiness in your life and make this programme activate more of that feel good factor, more energy so you feel all good things flowing throughout your body and mind. Great doesn't that feel great? Well it should do! You feel much better doing this, *don't you?* As you focus your attention on how your life is going to be in the future, build a mental bridge to get you there. So you see yourself in the future, more and more as the person you really want to be.

So now you know where you are at present and where you are going. You can bounce back when things don't go as you want them to. You focus on solutions, using your mind positively as you have been shown, changing problems into challenges, seeing your life in a positive light with enthusiasm and confidence. This is because now you are once again like you were as an infant, when you learnt to sit up, crawl, walk, stand up, run, talk and feed yourself. You are using all the resources you were born with confidence and persistence of purpose, courage, determination and all those other resources you used to achieve those life-changing tasks. You are not worrying about how or why, just doing it. Clicking on a computer in your brain is much easier than all that infant stuff, *well isn't it?* That **'can do' feeling** is now with you - so use it!

The Subconscious Mind Exercise

Read through the 'mind software' process and become very familiar with it. Then go through the relaxation process in chapter 4.

With your eyes closed go through the 'Mind Software Text' process by visualising it in your mind. As with all closed eye processes it needs to be done persistently to gain the maximum advantage from the process.

Place yourself in a safe, relaxed situation so you can focus on what you are doing and nothing else needs your attention.

NB. *Please remember* – **Because of the relaxation element in subconscious mind exercises, they should <u>never</u> be done when *you need to stay alert for some reason.***

PERCEPTIONS OF BELIEF

I was strolling through the woods one day thoroughly enjoying myself. It is probably the place in nature I am most happy and at peace. It was a wonderful warm day with a balmy breeze blowing and the fragrances of the wood around me. As I strolled along, an ocean of bluebells as far as the eye could see, opened up before me, a sight difficult to surpass in the whole of nature.

As I walked along the footpath through the woods, in the distance I noticed a man standing on a mound and he appeared to be pulling at the branches of a tree. It seemed a very destructive activity. As I walked towards the man I could see he was wearing a duffle coat with a hood pulled over his head. As I approached, I noticed he was a young man and I immediately thought it must be a hooligan vandalising a tree for the fun of it.

As I got closer to the 'tree destroyer' it certainly seemed he was pulling branches off the tree in what appeared to be a very indiscriminate way. I could see they were very tall beautiful pink flowering cherry trees, in full bloom and a stunning sight to behold. I approached even closer ready to tell this young hooligan exactly what I thought of him. He was obviously not someone pruning the tree in any structured way and he looked quite aggressive in his physical appearance and behaviour.

As I walked right up to him not really knowing what I would say or do, he suddenly disappeared down the other side of the mound out of my view, with what appeared to be a bunch of leaves and branches he had torn from the tree.

I went to the edge of the mound and looked down. There below, I saw a young girl in an invalid wheel chair. To my astonishment the young man was kneeling down in front of the girl handing her a bunch of flowering cherry tree blooms, which he had gathered from the tree. As he did so he gave her a loving peck on her cheek. In that moment I changed my hasty negative judgement to feelings of admiration, my eyes became watery and a tear dropped down. What a pure act of love I thought.

This episode reminded me of how we so often focus too closely on what we perceive as the negative aspects of others and ourselves when a wider more informed perspective might bring us closer to the truth.

It is the interpretation we put on feelings and situations that decides our response. Sometimes we need to experience something that moves our emotions positively in order to break out of our habitual negative perceptions.

> **It is not the situation that colours our experience but the way we look at it.**

CHAPTER ELEVEN: CREATING THE FUTURE YOU DESIRE.

When you accept yourself and life with a relaxed mind and body, the process of change becomes easier. This is as opposed to being full of tension, stressed, angry, critical and derisory about yourself and life in general. These negative feelings cause barriers and difficulties, inclined towards being your own worst enemy, instead of your own best friend!

When you accept how you are in the present, you place yourself in a very powerful position to create change. Living in the 'moment of now' is sound advice, but you also need to plan for the future. *If you had to visit a remote village in Scotland and you did not have a clue where it was or how to get there, what would you do?* There is surely only one answer; you would use a map or sat nav that showed you exactly where it is.

Planning effectively for your future is always a good activity to devote some of your time to. If you do not have clear definable goals short, medium and long term, then you will arrive somewhere in life - but it could be anywhere and almost certainly not where you want to be! So give yourself the opportunity to create a vision for your future. Look forward to a creative relationship with yourself as you continue on your new positive pathway.

Goals, goals, everyone is always on about goals. Goals are just things we want to change or things we want to achieve and we all have those desires, *don't you?* Think about the rest of your life in a constructive way. Take the opportunity to design the direction of your destiny and life. If you don't design your own life, chances are you'll fall into someone else's plan - and guess what they have planned for you? Not much. *Is that what you want?*

Asking the Right Questions

You can continue creating your new pathway into the future by answering these questions:
- *"What do I want from life?*
- *What are my needs so I can live a fulfilled life?*
- *What do I have to do to be happy, successful and at peace within myself?*
- *How can I interact with others in a completely free effective and* supportive *way?*
- *What do I want to do that I am not doing now?*
- *How will I motivate myself to achieve what I want in my life?*
- *What specific principles will I choose to believe in and act upon?*
- *Will my life be successful or having left too much to chance will I arrive somewhere I didn't plan and be dissatisfied?"*

Many questions but as you go through each one, focus on it, really think about it. As you go through this process a number of times and the questions are absorbed deeply into your subconscious mind, the answers often come from intuitive and creative sources within you. To get the process working at a conscious mind level too, make a written list of the main things you want to change and achieve. Questions are magnetic. The human mind naturally seeks answers that can rarely be ignored. Examine these at a conscious mind level and believe in you.

Do what inspires you most and observe the results in your life. Begin creating the new life you want to live. Act as if you already are the person you want to be. Decide exactly what it is you want. Be clear and positive. Visualise it, feel it, design it, hear it, touch it, taste it and above all **live it.**

You have previously read in this book how many people constantly think and dwell on what they don't want to happen in their lives. Remember how the mind works:

> **Whatever a person allows to persistently dwell in their mind with belief and conviction, they can manifest into their life.**

Always focus on what you want. Your subconscious mind will find a way. It will answer your questions with resolution and in many subtle ways.

However if you do what most people do, (that is look for obstacles and focus on how their life is not the way they want it to be) or ask:

"Why does everything go wrong for me?"

Your subconscious mind will search for the answer to that question and can only answer such a question in the same negative way. The answers may be: "I can't get things done because I am scared. I can't get things done because I fear failure. I am not educated enough. I haven't got enough money." If you consistently create negative statements about yourself you will consistently fail to achieve what you want. You will programme yourself to be a loser.

When you make a commitment to achieve what you want, you will be in the right frame of mind to get it. So be very clear on commitment.

> **Commitment is doing the thing you promised yourself to do, long after the mood when you first made the commitment has passed.**

One of the saddest things that can happen is to find yourself on your deathbed; lying there knowing you are dying and crying out "Is this really over? I haven't really started yet!" realising the awful truth: it is too late. All those great things you were going to do and never got around to doing. All your good intentions now dust in your mouth. Surely that motivates you to change now!

Time is of the Essence

Realise time is of the essence. There are many demands on your time.

If your life were ending now, what would your regrets be?

It is too late to write a 'to do' list then. Don't waste the time you have, you have it just once. Be a 'do it now' person. Your time is every breath you take: to eat, to sleep, to laugh, to play, to cry and to sink or swim. Don't watch it disappearing. Ask yourself:

"Do I want success in my life or disappointment?"

> **Being how you want to be means taking action, not dreaming and hoping.**

Getting what you want is about decisions and doing, making choices and taking responsibility for your life. When you know what you want, take action immediately, however small each step forward may be. Free yourself from the trivial and any constraints. The past is gone. Forget previous disappointments, the future is yet to come. Creating what you want in life is preparing for your future in advance. If you wait until a successful future might come along, it is too late. Then you are in the despair of: "If only I had done this, if only I had done that".

The fear of failure is often a reason people use not to do things. The-wait -and see way of living. "Let's just wait and see - I don't want to make any mistakes."

> **'Procrastination is the greatest thief of all time.'**

The truth is mistakes can be a positive part of life. Failure always presents the opportunity to learn, it should never be feared. We can even take what we think is a 'wrong turning' (make a mistake) and arrive at the right pathway- somewhere positive and beneficial, somewhere we never dreamt we could be. Although negative beliefs can appear very real, treat them as illusions. Enjoy your successes. Ask yourself success-orientated questions such as:

"How will it work? How will I be doing it?"
not:
"What will happen if I fail?"

Sometimes goals can seem difficult, life isn't always easy. *How can we ever learn if it is?*

It is so easy to allow other people to influence your self-belief negatively with their doubting critical words. Remember they can only put you off track if you allow them to. Always have in mind that opinions are like faces, they are all different and everyone has them but it doesn't make them right.

A Brighter Future

List all the benefits you will have when you are the person you want to be, coping with stress, negative mind chatter and other challenges you have to face in life. Motivating yourself will provide you with more mental and physical energy. See yourself as more pleasing and likeable to others, more confident, with greater feelings of self-esteem, self-liking and self-worth. So you can say with real belief:

"I am the person I want to be. I am who I am. I have the confidence to be me. My life is a better experience now than it ever was before. I can look in the mirror and see my best friend."

If you can believe that, with real conviction, you have changed forever.

Generate the positive attitude of mind that will empower you to achieve your unique destiny. If you consider all the benefits you desire, you will quickly notice that many of them you can have now. They are a choice you can make very quickly. It is amazing how realisation can change belief in a moment. It can be that potent and real.

Have you had the experience of feeling depressed and down, when suddenly somebody calls you with some really good news that really perks you up?

Whatever that news is, you instantaneously go from being really down, being low in energy and depressed, to all of a sudden lightening up. You feel much happier and all you did was pick up a phone and heard a voice.

Why wait for that to happen. Don't *wish* you were happy. Do more of the things that make you happy. Be happy now. The happiest people don't have everything they just make the best of everything they have.

Irrational fear is the greatest obstacle to becoming the person you want to be.

Frequently the fear does not even seem to have any reason attached to it. Often you cannot even identify what the fear is, you just feel it. Sometimes it's about letting the fear be there without having to attack it, without needing to analyse it to death. Don't call it stress, or any other name just because you don't like to acknowledge fear.

Be aware when fear is around. Don't pretend it's not there and try and brush it aside. Move forward in the face of fear. The fear then, wherever it comes from, loses its energy; it loses its power and force. If you feed the fear by allowing it to dwell negatively, it just grows more intense. Just carry on regardless of any fear.

Throughout this book you have given yourself the opportunity to go through, subconscious mind exercises, to remove outdated 'stop' signs that used to confine your behaviour to an unproductive zone of emotional uncertainty. You have greatly improved your emotional competence, enabling you to live your life in a more supportive and positive way.

You have made many behavioural, emotional and intellectual choices at various levels of consciousness. This has enabled you to access more and more of the template resources you were born with, that are deep within you that enable you to create the tangible skills you can use time and time again for your own personal advantage in achieving what you desire in your life. The mind processes you have read about and practiced in this book will help you progress into the future in a purposeful way. If used with persistence of purpose, the ideas and suggestions will enable you to accomplish all you need, to have the confidence to be you.

All you genuinely set your mind on, you can achieve. You can turn all your desires into solid, effective and long lasting changes. When you use imagination effectively and in a detached way you can guide your future actions with clear perspective and purpose. It really can be a useful and supportive resource to find you are getting more skilful at viewing things in a positive way. So go ahead and imagine everything that happens in the future has positive opportunities and possibilities. Really begin to live your life with that belief. You know now it's not the things that happen to you that matter but what you make of them. It is by logic you prove but by intuition you discover and change.

Give yourself permission, support and encouragement to succeed. As you realise everything you do is effectively creating your desired personal future, so you are developing your knowledge and skills for success.

You find it easier and easier to realise the many ways in which the real you emerges, with the confidence to believe everything will turn out well in the end. It just means that obstacles and difficulties are things to look at in a positive way, as challenges and not problems. You realise the potential that challenges contain and how you can ultimately prosper from anything that comes your way because you use your mind creatively and positively.

You can now step into a brighter future. Enjoy an awareness of the rich sources of information and resources within you and around you. You notice more of what will help you is there within you. You can live with a relaxed awareness, strengthened by the support of all you learn, helping you respond decisively to the things you desire to change and the things you want to achieve.

Every response you make and every action you take produces an outcome closer to what you want to achieve and further away from what you want to leave behind. Your awareness and focus gives you perspective.

> **The experience you require for success comes from interacting with life and taking action.**

Creativity and persistence are resources available to help you proceed as you observe your continued learning and success. Remember anytime you sense a stuck state, release whatever is causing it and let the stress flow away. Prevent the pushing and pulling of the past in your body and in your mind. Relax and be receptive. Notice the rich abundant information and support all around you and within you, guiding your breakthrough to greater and greater success.

You know what you want, don't you? So go forward with a strong purpose and clear aims in mind, taking action in a purposeful direction towards what you want to achieve. Witness the outcomes you produce and remain persistent until you achieve what you desire. Steadily proceeding along towards successful outcomes is becoming an automatic part of your approach to life's challenges.

Release negativity and achieve the successful outcomes you desire. Become more aware of the wisdom within you. The more you become aware of this inner wisdom and its gentle guidance, the more you'll realise how you always have this friend within - getting more competent every day at spotting the many subtle ways your subconscious mind communicates with you.

It's such a joy to know that you have access to something within you, something you carry with you, wherever you go. You have this intuition that's always been there. You might wonder just how you'll start paying closer attention to how it can guide you. Your pathway forward then becomes clearer and clearer as your life flows along, like a river being supplied by many small streams, flowing around boulders and obstacles until it flows into the sea and then ever forward into a mighty ocean of possibilities. Well that's a natural thing to happen. *Well isn't it?*

Your Book of Life

So now may I suggest you imagine you are flipping through your book of life. You know how, with a thumb on the slightly spread out pages. Flip those pages so rapidly, so that each page is only a blink of the eye. Every single idea and suggestion in the book flips into your mind - all the positive meanings that are uniquely useful to you. Your subconscious mind can do this at a speed and clarity your conscious mind is quite incapable of doing. So your subconscious mind becomes fully aware of the person you can be in the future... now.

> **Your intuition is a powerful tool for change – use it!**

Your conscious mind can only take in about seven to nine pieces of information at one time, whereas your subconscious mind can handle millions of pieces of information all at once. Think how it runs every single thing that goes on in your body, from breathing to constantly re-creating the cells in your body and doing all the wonderful things that go on in your body every minute of your life. So allow all the knowledge and understanding that is just right for you, flow into every single cell in your body, so it is there for you to use now and in the future. How and in what way you want to use it is always your choice. So why not enjoy a sense of security and with an indestructible belief that whatever happens, come what may, you can cope. You can meet any obstacle in your life and overcome it and meet any challenge and enjoy facing it.

It can also be a learning curve to come up against situations you find difficult to handle and then later, think it over and fully realise they too were learning experiences in many supportive, useful and different ways. Such challenges allow you to discover those areas of your life of which you need more experience. You can use your self-belief and a real sense of security, which rests comfortably within you, so you react to good or bad, dealing with it all in a constructive way.

Imagine you are flipping through the pages of the book of your future life. Notice how your quest for happiness, success and fulfilment progresses in the book. Whatever you see in your book is what you have been focusing on ever since you started out on your pathway towards becoming the person you want to be. Flipping through your book those ideas and suggestions that are especially relevant and important to you will come into your mind. You will know they are important because they come from your mind in an entirely intuitive way, so that all is coming from within. Flip through the pages several times.

Each time you flip quickly through the book you might have the same ideas to review or new ideas to work with. When you have completed the process on many occasions over a period of time, you will have reviewed the most important information, ideas and suggestions from the book that you can place particular emphasis on, in order to work effectively on your road towards happiness, success and fulfilment... knowing you can always perform better outside, when the knowledge about you inside is true.

Subconscious Mind Exercise

Now close your eyes and go through the relaxation process in chapter 4. Then, in your imagination, flip through your future book of life as described above. Feel how absolutely fabulous it is to be really happy, not just at the odd moment, but most of the time. Imagine fear disappearing from your life, feeling confident and moving forward overcoming any obstacle foolish enough to get in your way. Think clearly and positively, being a lot more creative in your thinking, ideas flow more easily. Your direction in life is clear and positive. You are more creative. You are more willing to try new things, taking more risks and the changes you want to make already achieved, your relationships flourishing in a successful and positive way. You cope with stress without thinking about it. Life is fun and exciting. If, at any stage you would like a closer look at a particular event, stop and observe the event more closely. Do this many times until you clearly see your future pathway in life as you want it to be. A lot of what you desire will be subconsciously observed, then brought into conscious awareness when it is appropriate to do so. Remember aerodynamically a bumblebee should not be able to fly. Fortunately bumblebees don't know this, so they just fly.

NB. *Please remember* - **Because of the relaxation element in the subconscious mind exercises, they should <u>never</u> be done when** *you need to stay alert for some reason.*

SEARCHING FOR SHANGRI-LA

Once upon a time a young man heard about the story of Shangri-la. A mysterious stranger told him a land exists beyond the highest mountains in the world, in a secret valley hidden by a ring of snow-capped mountains, which guard the gateway to the kingdom of Shangri-la; a utopia where all people had everything that was possible to have.

"I must search for this wonderful place. I must find it", thought the young man. So he set off to search for this paradise. He passed through great wastelands of ice and severe cold and travelled across the most terrible terrain that could ever be imagined without finding the utopia he was seeking.

The young man finally came across an old hermit living in a cave who asked him. "Where are you going to through this inhospitable land?"

"To find Shangri-la", the young man boldly replied.

"Then I can help you", replied the hermit. "When you come to the crystal mountain you will find a terrifying demon called 'Flashing Lightening'. The demon will entice you to the luxury beyond and split the crystal mountain asunder to let you pass by, where you will find a place of great wealth and every material luxury you could ever wish for. However you must first give your allegiance to the demon." As the young man continued his journey, out of the mist ahead appeared an ethereal spiritual figure. "What are you seeking?" asked the apparition.

"I seek paradise on earth - a place of great wealth and all kind of material luxuries," the young man replied.

"You will never find what you need there, for a healthy, happy, successful and fulfilled life," responded the celestial figure. "The knowledge and wisdom of truth and happiness cannot be obtained from the material world.

"Why not?" The young man angrily retorted, and asked. "Well where can I find it?"

"The wisdom you seek only exists in the mind and spirit of people. You can only find it through the unlimited possibilities of the human mind. Listen to the following and it should help you:

For every person there is a way. The correct thinker climbs the high way. The flawed thinker gropes the low. In between on the misty flats, the rest drift to and fro. But to every person there opens a way and each person can <u>decide the way their life shall go."</u>

"Well how do I find the right way for me?" asked the young man.

"To do that you must quieten your mind and be in peace, then examine your most profound beliefs and feelings. Make effective contact with your subconscious mind, that most intimate part of you. There alone can you find the true Shangri-la. You do not need to suffer bodily or mental strife to seek that which you desire. It can be achieved, effortlessly, comfortably and positively. All you need is persistence of purpose."

So the young man knew this was the pathway to go along to find his personal Shangri-la. There wasn't any other way. As he followed his own pathway the young man learnt many things. He began to accept defeats with his head held high and his eyes open and to do so with the grace of an adult, not with the petulance of a child. If things went wrong he now knew it didn't mean he wasn't any good, it just meant nobody was perfect.

So he learnt to build all his future pathways in life on his own profound beliefs and discovered every situation is a learning process when he allowed it to be so. So he stopped looking for Shangri-la outside there somewhere. He decided to plant his own garden and decorate his own soul, instead of waiting for someone to bring him flowers. He then learnt he really could endure, that he really was special; he did have self-worth, self-respect and self-liking. So he began to live and know himself and in doing so, started living a life of success, happiness and fulfilment. And so it was.

CHAPTER TWELVE: USING THE MENTAL LAWS OF SUCCESS POSITIVELY

Ask yourself the following questions:

- "What do *I need to do to have –The confidence to be me? (This is the most important question of all to ask)*
- *How can I understand myself better?*
- *How can I be happier?*
- *How can I make my life more interesting and meaningful?*
- *How can I bring more purpose into my life?*
- *What do I really consider to be success in my life?*
- *How can I fulfil my own personal and unique needs?"*

Imagine the empowerment it gives you for the future, as you answer these questions positively and how quickly you can action your conclusions by using 'The Mental Laws of Success.'

One of the things you're going to love about all you learn from this book is the feeling of power and control you'll have in influencing your life.

YOU CAN PROGRAMME YOUR MIND FOR FAILURE OR SUCCESS THE CHOICE IS YOURS.

Subconscious Mind Exercise

Make sure you are in a relaxed, comfortable situation so your focus is on what you are doing and nothing else needs your attention. Go through the Mental Laws of Success, make sure you are well acquainted with what they mean and how you can use them in your life.

Read through the relaxation process described in chapter 4, pages 37-40.

Then with closed eyes go through the relaxation process in your mind once more and visualise the scenes described in the relaxation text. Then go back to an event in the past that did not happen as you wanted it to. Use whichever of the 'Mental Laws of Success' you need to reframe the memory, so you achieve a new successful outcome.

Now go into the future and see yourself in a similar situation performing and feeling exactly how you want to.

Once you feel you have satisfactorily re-framed one situation you can go on to others until all those past unsatisfactory memories and experiences have been turned into successful ones and you have also recreated them for positive future experiences as well.

This can be a very successful way of using your mind, simply because the subconscious mind does not have any sense of time. Whatever you are thinking it believes is happening in the present. That means you can reframe the past and create positive expectations for the future and do it all now.

NB. *Please remember* - Because of the relaxation element in the subconscious mind exercises they should <u>never</u> be done when *you need to stay alert for some reason.*

CHAPTER THIRTEEN: DETACHMENT

The concept of using 'Mental Detachment' to achieve personal change is not always easy to understand. The 'subconscious mind exercises' contained in this book best illustrate the use of 'detachment' when engaged in mental activity.

The process of detachment in many ways goes against the generally recognised idea of the road to success, 'the toil sweat and tears' way that is often necessary when endeavouring to achieve a physical goal. With mental goals there is another far more effective way, one that will lead you away from the pathway of stress, anxiety and fear. It means you do not follow any specific way as the only pathway towards achievement.

'Detachment' is a powerful process in bringing about personal change, by releasing your intenseness about any mental activity you engage in. It is often difficult for you to appreciate this quieter, more relaxed way. In the past you have probably done it the hard way, by gritting your teeth and hyping yourself up, using the black and white way of thinking one example being the 'no pain, no gain' kind of mentality. This may be advantageous in any physical endeavour but it certainly isn't the best way to achieve any mental task.

Relinquishing your attachment to what you desire doesn't mean you give up your intention to achieve it. You don't give up the intention and you certainly do not diminish your desire. You just give up your attachment to a specific way of reaching your goal. You reject 'it must be done this way; this is the only way to do it;' putting yourself in a straight jacket without the choice to adapt as you go along.

'Detachment' is a very powerful process to use. The moment you relinquish your attachment to a specific result you can combine flexibility with intention. Anything can be achieved because it is based on self-belief - not necessarily following the way others say it should be done.

The opposite of 'detachment' is attachment. All that 'have to', 'must do', 'should do', and 'ought to do', causes pressure, anxiety and fear, based on feelings of insecurity. This is putting yourself down with negative self-criticism and frustration because you can't change by following the generally accepted way of doing things. The need for security comes from not knowing the self – not knowing what your true needs are. Most people, when they try to achieve their goals in life, have a tendency to chase symbols that come and go. Chasing symbols is like settling for a map instead of the actual territory. It creates anxiety; it ends up making you feel hollow and empty inside.

You can become attached to what you want to change, allowing learned limitations to reinforce rigid behaviour by repeating old sequences and response patterns. Doing the same old thing over and over again, in a very rigid sort of way, you create resistance to change. Then you find it more and more difficult to step beyond the boundaries you are attached to. I once read that the definition of unsuccessful is doing the same thing again and again and expecting a different result.

I used 'detachment' as a way of directing my thinking when I became disillusioned with my job in the commercial world. I detached myself from my attachment to the job I had and the money I earned from it and asked myself these questions:

"What do I need to change to meet my real needs; what would bring me genuine happiness?"

Of course a great deal of deliberation took place to answer these questions. The result was I made my decision in a detached, relaxed and clear-headed way to leave my job in the commercial world and become a stress therapist

We rarely examine our behaviour to find out if it is working for us or against us. We just keep trying to reap crops for which we have never sown the seeds. We rarely question our attitudes or why we hold the opinions we have. I have met so many people who give no other reason why they think and act and behave in certain ways other than that was what their mother or father did.

At this point I am reminded of the newly married man who was watching his wife prepare the Sunday joint. He saw her do something that to him seemed quite strange. She chopped the ends of the joint before she placed it in the roasting tray.

"Curious," he thought and asked his wife: "Why do you cut the ends off the joint before putting it into the roasting tray?"

"Because that is how my mother does it, his wife replied." The next time he visited his wife's mother he asked. "If it is not a rude question, could you tell me why you cut the ends off a joint of meat before you put it into the roasting tray?"

"Because that's how my mother did it", his mother-in-law replied. The man knew his wife's mother lived in the granny flat attached to the house. So he popped in to see her. "I am really consumed with curiosity" he said. "Both your daughter and granddaughter cut the ends of the joint before they roast it. Do you know why?"

"Oh! They don't still do that? I did it because I only had one roasting tray and couldn't afford a new one. I had to cut the ends off so it would fit into the tray."

This tale illustrates how our behaviour can become habitual. We rarely think of being detached from what we do and ask *"Why do I do that?"*

> **In the future why not step outside your usual comfort zones and do some things differently? Then enjoy the beneficial results of doing so.**

A detached attitude gives you the freedom to create. You can then be involved in what you are doing with a sense of adventure. What you want to change tends to come about spontaneously and effortlessly. Without 'detachment' you can become a prisoner of mundane needs, trivial concerns and quiet desperation. You can get caught up in what can be a mediocre habitual existence, separated from creativity and change.

You are probably constantly seeking security. However security is a very transient thing. When you seek security in everything you do, you can do it for a lifetime without ever finding it. 'Detachment' uses the wisdom of insecurity and the uncertainty of the unknown. Seeking certainty and security is an attachment to the known. The known is the past. The known is nothing other than living in a prison of past conditioning. There isn't any evolution in that. When there is no evolution, there is stagnation and disorder and even chaos.

'Detachment' from what you want to change about yourself and your life is the fertile ground of pure creativity and freedom. It means stepping into the unknown, the field of all possibilities, always open to new things happening. Every day you can look for the excitement of what may occur that is new in your life. When you come across uncertainty, don't give up; you are on the right path. You don't need a complete rigid idea of what you'll be doing next week, next month or next year. If you have a very rigid idea of what's going to happen and get attached to it, you overlook a whole range of possibilities of what could happen. If you become attached, your intention can get locked into a rigid mindset, which can lead to an inflexibility that interferes with your creative processes.

When I was young my favourite colours were black and white. I use to draw a lot of black and white pictures in Indian ink. The black and white world was fine for me. I even won prizes for it at school. In due time I learnt that black and white were in fact not colours. This opened my mind to the magic and wonder of a rainbow and how from these primary colours, thousands of other colours could be created. It taught me the black and white way of looking at life could be restricting my potential in opening up many other avenues of challenging and exciting discoveries and opportunities. I had received recognition for my black and white pictures but the rewards I gained from the multi-coloured pathways I took later in life were far more satisfying than prizes placed in my hand for all to see. They were rewards I felt in my heart and soul.

> **Enjoy discovering that you really can be flexible enough to respond differently.**

The more you use the 'Detachment' process, the more you find out how you can use your natural abilities and skills to respond in more flexible ways. Learn how to release the usual tension and stress. Evolve a relaxed way of doing things. Change the old patterns of thinking that haven't worked in the past. Change discomfort to comfort. Discover new possibilities in old situations, in ways that make you feel good at all levels of your mind and body.

Allow yourself different responses in situations where it would be most helpful to do so. Open the door to new possibilities and close the door on outdated ways of trying to achieve – ways that have only in the past caused you tension and stress. Day by day, use 'Detachment' as a new approach to your life, instead of the old 'do or die' methods. Use the detached, relaxed way. You will be amazed how it will change your life in many different ways.

It should always be realised that 'Detachment' does not interfere with your desire and intention of achieving what you want or how you want to change. You still have a direction in which to go and goals to achieve. However make it a journey of discovery rather than a meticulously mapped territory. On your journey towards your goals, between departure and arrival, there are always infinite possibilities if you are open to them.

With a detached attitude you can always change direction at any moment and find another way, perhaps more exciting and more rewarding than you thought possible. You are unlikely to try and force solutions on problems just change them into challenges. This enables you to stay alert to opportunities that are always there. This state of alertness prepares you to seize opportunities instead of missing out on them.

Many people try to avoid uncertainty and create a safety zone they are reluctant to move away from. However every problem you have in your life represents a seed of opportunity to open up a whole range of new possibilities. If you think of everything you want to change in your life as a challenge, this motivates you to live your life as an adventure and not a predictable safe journey.

> **Detachment allows time for mystery, wonder, excitement and motivation to be an important part of your life.**

Good luck and bad luck are often spoken about as part of life which people generally believe they do not have much control over. Rarely true! Good luck is mainly nothing more than awareness and opportunity coming together. A solution emerges and if it is from a subconscious creative source you may not even realise where it comes from. This is often looked upon as 'Good Luck.'

'Detachment' from what you desire is a belief that you can achieve what you desire, in due time, whenever that may be. The following words can be used as affirmations to commit you to 'detachment' as a process for achievement.

- I allow my desires and goals the freedom to happen in due time.
- I avoid rigidly imposing specific ideas on how I should achieve any change I desire.
- I participate in everything with detached involvement.
- I avoid rigidly forcing solutions to problems, as this only creates more problems.
- I accept uncertainty as an essential ingredient in any experience.
- In my willingness to accept uncertainty, I change problems into challenges and create

spontaneous solutions that can emerge from confusion, disorder and even chaos.
- The more uncertain things seem to be, the more secure I feel. Uncertainty is my pathway to freedom.
- With the freedom of uncertainty my life remains open to infinite opportunities.
- In detachment lies the wisdom of uncertainty … in the wisdom of uncertainty lays the freedom from my past - from the known, which is the prison of my past conditioning. My willingness to step into the unknown and consider all possibilities enables me to use my creative mind, which then orchestrates my pathway in life.

Working Effectively with your Subconscious Mind.

It is now time to use your subconscious mind. Let your conscious mind do whatever it wants to do. It can pay attention if it wants to – and probably it will, because the conscious mind is always very curious about what's going on – it always wants to know things. So probably it will want to stay alert. However it may go off on a daydream of its own or have its attention diverted by this or that. If it does, just let it go - because it is time once again to give the subconscious mind some work to do.

You have already discovered through practice and experience, a good and satisfying way to relax, reaching deeper levels of relaxation, having found out just how quickly you can guide your mind and body into a deep level of comfort within yourself. (See chapter 4.) So now select some change you want to make about yourself that you habitually do, which in the past you have tried to change in the old intense stressful, anxiety driven way, the way that rarely works. Then in a calm detached manner go exploring through the past and present, perhaps even the future. Search for information that could be useful for you to change in the way you want. Leave your subconscious mind to gather information, sift through it, filter it and organise it, to present it to your conscious mind at appropriate times and in appropriate ways.

> **Start thinking about things from a slightly different angle and wonder why you did not think in this way before.**

New ideas, new patterns of thinking are developed in subtle ways. You get glimpses of how 'Detachment' works; by creating this new calm 'go with the flow' approach to the changes you want to make. These changes about your life are made without the old tension and stress element present.

You allow your subconscious mind to re-evaluate old thinking and behaviour from the past that is interfering with your present attempts to change. Remember when you were a very young child and you looked up at a house and it seemed so big, when trees along the roadside or in the park looked so tall and many of those hills you looked at seemed so steep. Eventually, when you became older you realised the house or building you thought was so huge was in fact quite ordinary and it might even have been on the small side. The tree was in fact just an ordinary-sized tree and the hill, quite a gentle slope. You looked at things with a different perspective. They were different to you as an adult, because you were able to put them in proper perspective.

In the same way, you can guide your subconscious mind to re-evaluate old patterns of thinking and behaviour. Realise that your subconscious mind started these patterns at an early stage in your life, believing they were valid and possibly even necessary. They now need reassessing. Many of them have become out of date, so it is time for them to be revised, resolved and modified; brought up to date so they are suitable to help you in your life now.

Subconscious Mind Exercise

To use the process of detachment to help you change in the way you want, allow your subconscious mind to choose a specific aspect of yourself you want to change. Consciously you may think you know what it is but your subconscious mind has so much more information than your conscious mind. Your subconscious mind may know of some behavioural change that needs to be taken care of first. So take several deep breaths in and out and spend a few moments deciding on the change you want to make.

Now focus your mind on the specific change you have chosen, by visualising yourself how you want to be. Create some visual pictures of yourself in a situation as the changed 'you' – behaving, thinking and feeling exactly how you want.

If you feel any 'must do' tension, release it. While you are doing this, your subconscious mind will extract in a calm way, the information it needs, then it will change what needs to be changed and will guide you to do what is necessary for the change to happen. As you go through this process a number of times, some things will seem easier for you. You won't be bothered as much as you used to be. You will think of new ways to handle the old negative behaviour. This will smooth the way and point out new directions - changing one small thing after another until the change is complete.

You can now, in this comfortable relaxed and detached way, learn what you need to know and know what you need to learn. When you do this with persistence of purpose you will be amazed how easy it is **for you to change.**

Having made yourself familiar with the above **'detachment'** process, relax down as you have done previously - chapter 4, pages 37-40. Go through the process of imagining yourself living your life in this **new 'detached' way**. Like all other subconscious mind exercises, repetition and persistence of purpose are important.

NB. *Please remember* - Because of the relaxation element in the subconscious mind exercises they should <u>never</u> be done when *you need to stay alert for some reason.*

USING POSITIVE SELF TALK

THE FOLLOWING POSITIVE PHRASES FREQUENTLY REPEATED, WITH CONVICTION AND BELIEF CAN BE THE KEYS TO OPENING NEW DOORS IN YOUR LIFE:

➢ No person or any thought action or experience can cause me any harm, stress or anxiety unless I allow it to.
➢ I remember always that it is not people, situations or experiences that cause me anxiety or stress but my perceptions of them.
➢ I empower myself with self-belief. My self-belief guides me forward positively, no matter where life may lead.
➢ Whatever convictions and beliefs I allow to dwell persistently in my mind, I can manifest into my life.
➢ I believe that hate destroys but love and forgiveness heals.
➢ I recognise it is not the situation that defines any experience but the way I look at it.
➢ Whatever I believe with feeling and desire can become my reality
➢ I know when I am doing things right for me because I feel freedom, security and peace.
➢ Whatever I expect to happen with my own performance, either negative or positive, generally does happen.

➢ I know that persistence of purpose is the only way to succeed. So I keep carrying on until I am the person I want to be and have achieved all I want to achieve.

➢ For every effect in my life there is a specific cause. I have the ability to control the causes and change the effects to anything I want.

➢ My thoughts are the primary cause of the conditions and effects in my life. If I want my life to be different in the future I have to change my thinking in the present.

➢ I feel good about myself to the degree to which I am in control of my life. I feel out of harmony with myself to the degree to which I allow other people and circumstances to control me.

➢ One short life is soon past. Only that done <u>with love</u> will last.

➢ Every day I get closer and closer to the life of success and happiness I desire.

HOW YOU CAN GAIN THE MAXIMUM BENEFIT FROM THIS BOOK

To gain lasting benefits from this book it is necessary to use what you have learnt actively and consistently in your everyday life. Use it as a long-term reference book.

Keep carrying out the subconscious mind exercises over and over again for maximum benefit, especially the ones that work well for you. You will discover new ideas and new inspiration on many levels of consciousness. This cannot be emphasised enough.

Too many people gain very useful knowledge but then do not put into practice what they have learnt. What a waste of time and money that is. Please do not make the mistake of just using this book as an interesting one-off experience. It is so much more than that. It is a way of using your mind that will effectively support you as a powerful psychological tool for positive change in so many different ways, for the rest of your life.

People often create disappointment in their life because they only think, talk or dream about how they want to be and what they want to do with their life. The secret of a successful and happy life is self-awareness and deciding what you really want to do with your life. Decide what you want first then live your life achieving it. Too many lives are littered in later years by a whole string of: "If only I had done this, if only I had done that," instead of being the person you really want to be and doing the things you really want to do. That means having the confidence to be you.

> *"Concerning all acts of achievement there is one elementary truth. The moment you definitely make a genuine commitment to start, all sorts of things occur to help you that would not otherwise have happened. A whole stream of positive events and issues go in your favour. All manner of unforeseen incidents and good fortune comes your way. <u>Whatever you can do or dream, you can begin. Boldness has genius and power in it. Begin it now.</u>"*
>
> (Translated from a quotation by Johann Wolfgang von Goethe).

The only real measure of personal success is the quality of the journey, not the final destination - for we all arrive at the same destination in the end. Happiness is our birthright it is not conditional on what has happened to us, or what material things we have acquired in life. You really can open up your life for change as you consider the benefits this book can bring you.

The final value of this book to you will depend on how much of the insights, advice and guidance you choose to adopt as routine ways of thinking and acting for the rest of your life. Various alternative processes for change are contained in the book. Try them all - then continue to do the ones that work best for you.

It will be beneficial to read the book more than once. Even the most intelligent, thoughtful reader needs to go through this book several times to be able to pick up, think over and internalise all the ideas suggested.

Each repeated reading will spark off additional ideas that apply to your needs and aspirations. The choice of course is yours!

Focused Learning

Set aside a short period each day for going through one of the 'Subconscious Mind Exercises.' This is the easiest way for focused assimilation and learning in a creative way. Many people expect to solve emotional problems by looking outwards first. The right way is to look in before you look out. Do not look outside yourself for the truth about you, your truth can only be found within you.

Write Down Your Ideas

Use your notepad questionnaire. Keep a notebook at hand and be prepared to stop reading at any time when you come across an idea or suggestion that particularly appeals to you. Think about the idea. Link it up with any connection it has with your family, social or work life. Note how it can be of special value to you, how it could change and improve your current thinking and behaviour. Work out how you can apply it in your life now. Make some notes to remind yourself of your new thinking so it can alert you to take action during the days and weeks ahead. A personal diary or lined notepad would be a good place to keep your notes in.

Turn Diary Notes into Positive Action

Until you do things effectively to change your thinking and the way you live your life, little or nothing will be accomplished. So once you have grasped an idea and you have decided this is for you, introduce it into your daily life. Sometimes the results may seem slow in coming. However if you are determined, persistent and courageous, you'll soon discover you are able to make the changes you desire and develop a more successful life by using the creative ways suggested in this book.

When you persistently start telling and showing your subconscious mind (visualising) how you want to be, in due course, it brings many ideas of value and importance into your conscious thinking. You will then start to manifest what you think into your life.

The subconscious mind is like a chrysalis, similar to the wonder of nature being able to produce a beautiful butterfly. All you have to do is keep feeding it with positive thoughts and actions. If you do that persistently, it crystallises them and helps you become the person you want to be.

Post Script...
This book is a compilation of the basic therapy I have successfully used for over twenty years with the clients who came to me for help. If you are committed and persistent in using these same ideas, you can change in ways that in the past you have probably only dreamt about.

NOTEPAD QUESTIONNAIRE

Chapter Six

"Am I entirely happy with my life now, if not why?"

"What do I need to change so my life can be happy and successful?"

"How do I need to change to become the person I really want to be?"

"What are my beliefs about me? Do I need to challenge some of them in order to change?"

"What do I want to do now?"

Chapter Seven

"Do I blame other people for how I feel act and behave? How do I need to change to *stop doing this?*"

"When hurtful experiences from the past keep giving me negative experiences in the present what can I do to stop this happening?"

"How can I get more joy in my life by just being me?"

"Do I still have issues with my parents, relatives or friends and how can I resolve these?"

Chapter Eight

"Are there any significant actions of forgiveness I need to deal with and what action do I need to take to solve these issues?"

"Are there any instances in my life when I did not receive unconditional love when I expected to receive it? What can I do to rid myself of hurtful feelings this causes me?"

"How can I introduce more humour into situations that I have previously reacted to by feeling depressed and stressed about?"

"How can I turn things that go wrong in my life to my advantage by learning from them?"

Chapter Nine

"How can I deal with any 'abundance' issues I have in my life?"

"I can decide what my precise 'abundance' needs are, write them down and take positive action to achieve them."

Chapter Ten

"Am I happy to be me or are there some aspects of myself I want to change? If so I will make a list of the changes I want to make and start taking positive action about them without any further delay."

"Am I contented with the quality of my life? If not I can write down an action plan as to how I can improve it."

"Do I need the approval of other people to make me feel good about myself? If so I need to do something about this."

Chapter Eleven

"What do I need to do to be happy, successful and live a fulfilled life?"

"If my life was ending now what regrets would I have, what specifically are they and what action can I take to ensure I do not end my life with a list of things I wanted to do but didn't get round to doing them?"

"Am I in the position when I am just waiting for something to happen? Do I believe procrastination is the greatest thief of all time?" What can I do to take some action on a daily basis to bring about the changes I desire?"

"Do I want my book of life to be positive and successful? If I do I need to stop wasting my time hoping and dreaming otherwise I could end up somewhere but not where I want to be."

Chapter 12

"How can I use the 'mental laws' to help overcome specific problems and challenges in my life?"

CONCLUSION

To conclude I would like to leave you with these thoughts:

ONE SHORT LIFE SOON WILL PASS, ONLY THAT DONE WITH LOVE WILL LAST

When I read these words for the first time, over forty years ago, it made me realise that happiness in life isn't about the never ending pursuit of material possessions, a larger house, bigger car, expensive holidays or any other material possession we seek from the world around us

> **Only that which comes from within can guide you on your personal journey towards success and happiness.**

In an ever-changing universe of pulsating energy there cannot be an absolute truth. Each truth must be effective for you. So always feel free to do what you believe works for you.

> **That which lies behind us and whatever may lie before us, are small matters in comparison to the potential that lies within us. So go ahead and achieve your own personal pathway towards happiness and success. By using this book you can achieve it much sooner than you may have ever imagined possible.**

> 'Everything can be taken from a man but one thing: the last of human freedoms – to choose one's attitude to any given set of circumstances, to choose one's own way.'
> Victor Frankel.

ABOUT THE AUTHOR

Before becoming a professional therapist, Michael worked for many years in the commercial world, in shipping and freight forwarding. For the last 8 years in the business world, before Michael trained as a therapist, he was the UK representative of The International Leipzig Trade Fair, at the time, arguably the largest trade fair in the world. In the 1980's he organised through the patronage of Lord Ted Willis, a reception for The Leipzig Fair in The House of Lords. This is the only occasion, to Michael's knowledge, that a trade fair has ever held a reception in this illustrious and historic setting. He dealt with many 'Blue Chip' companies and Government departments concerned with international trade, including The Department for Trade & Industry. His commercial professional qualifications include: Fellow of The Institute of Freight Forwarders, Member of The Institute of Chartered Shipbrokers and a Member of The British Institute of Management.

For most of his commercial career Michael travelled overseas frequently. This varied environment helped him to gain a vast experience of life and the stress involved. He does not consider spending many years in the commercial world before he became a professional therapist any disadvantage at all. On the contrary, he considers it a great advantage, as it provided him with a wide experience of life that no amount of academic study of psychology or psychotherapy could have ever provided.

Having studied techniques of stress control and self-development psychology for his own benefit, Michael became increasingly motivated to pass on to other people what he had learnt and after some deliberation, decided to leave the commercial world and train as a professional therapist.

After becoming professionally qualified in stress management Michael started his therapy practice as a stress therapist in Rochester, Kent. Shortly afterwards he was invited by the seven resident GPs at the Gun Lane Medical centre in Strood, Rochester, to become their Medical Practice Stress Therapist.

In the 1990s, Michael, together with a long-term cancer patient Robert Mayes, started 'The Medway Centre for Cancer Support and Care.' A number of complementary therapists were involved with this project.

In September 2002 he started working at the 'Integrated Care Centre' in Longfield, Kent. Michael was one of the original therapists who helped develop this 'flagship centre' into the successful enterprise it now is.

In December 2003 Michael was appointed one of the original members of the 'Public and Patient Involvement Forum' working in partnership with The Medway National Health Trust and Medway Maritime Hospital. He is an Associate Member of The Royal Society of Medicine and is registered with The Complementary and Natural Health Care Council (CNCH), the UK regulator for complementary healthcare.

Positions held past & present include:
Member of the Ethics & Disciplinary Committee of the Society of Stress Therapists.

Member of the Joint Training Committee of the Society of Stress Therapists and WellMind Training

A Director of WellMind Training Ltd.

A Director of the Council of the Society of Stress Therapists.

Coordinator for the Southern Region of The Society of Stress Therapists.

Editor of the Journal of Stress Management.

Ph.D. – Doctor of Philosophy (Hon).

Professional Qualification: Fellow and life member of the Society of Stress Managers (FSSM).

GLOSSARY

Adult ego: Part of the mind that reacts to reality and has a sense of individuality.
Affirmations: Statements spoken in a positive way.
Alpha relaxed state of mind: When attention is focused to achieve an alert and calm concentration.
Behavioural: Relating to behaviour.
Bio-chemical change: The creation of new chemical-induced coding in the mind.
Conscious mind: That part of thinking and behaviour a person is informed about or has knowledge of.
Consciousness: The totality of a person's thoughts and feelings:
Creative mind: That part of thinking that is original, inventive and imaginative.
Effective Outcomes: Achieving sound or acceptable results.
Ego: Part of the mind that reacts to reality and has a sense of individuality.
Emotional abandonment: When a person is emotionally detached from another, whether intentionally or not.
Emotional challenges: The events in life when a person is faced with spontaneous rather than rational experiences causing agitation and disturbance of the mind.
Emotional competence: The ability to cope with one's own and other people's emotions.
Emotional intelligence: The genuine knowledge a person has of human emotions and the use they can make of this learning to help themselves and other people in an understanding and supportive way.
External forces: Circumstances and situations in the world.

Feedback cycle: Gathering information from things a person has done and experienced.
Goals: The objective of a person's ambition and effort.
Human Givens: Innate resources that help people to meet their basic needs.
Ingenious survivor: A person who can overcome extreme adversity.
Inner dialogue: The words and thoughts that pass through our minds.
Internal critic: Self-criticism. When a person finds fault in what they have said or how they have behaved.
Intuition: An immediate insight without conscious reasoning.
Intuitive: When a person understands something immediately without any prior reasoning.
Invalid beliefs and behaviour: Beliefs and behaviour that are created by a conditional response but are not authentic or true.
Inward focus: When a person is focussed only on his/her own thoughts and feelings.
Limiting beliefs and behaviour: Beliefs and behaviour that challenge a person's ability to achieve.
Material stereotypes: Standardized possessions that society dictates a person must have to be recognised as being successful.
Mental laws: Psychological laws or rules that govern the basic way the human mind operates.
Mind chatter: Self-talk generally frivolous and meaningless.
Mind energy: The human mind's force, vigour, verve, zest and capacity for activity.
Mind tools: Exercises for using the mind in an effective and positive way.
Mindset: Habits of the mind formed by earlier events or experiences

Natural creativity: The innate ability of the human mind to be inspired, inventive and imaginative.

Negative Trance: A focused state of attention on pessimistic thoughts and feelings

Neurological pathways: The way the mind sends messages throughout the nervous system using electrical and chemical impulses.

Psychological well-being: Being in a state of peace and harmony.

Re-framed: The way an event is changed by altering how it is perceived for example when a liability is changed into an asset or a negative into a positive.

Resources: The means available to achieve positive results.

Self-actualisation: A feeling one is becoming all one is capable of becoming.

Self-attack: Self-criticism that adversely affects a person's confidence and self-esteem.

Self-awareness: Having an intimate knowledge of one's own individuality and basic character.

Self-belief: A person's trust and confidence in his/her self.

Self-fulfilling prophecy: The likelihood that what we genuinely expect to happen will happen.

Self-talk: The internal conversation people have in their mind especially in regard to the way they describe themselves.

Special place: Picturing a place in your mind that is unique and special to you.

Self-worth: Having a favourable opinion of oneself.

State: The condition or position of a person.

Stuck state: When a person is in a static psychological condition.

Stress: The demand on physical or mental energy. The reaction people have to an imbalance they perceive to be placed upon them and the resources they have to cope.

Stress response: A person's interpretation of an event that causes debilitating symptoms.

Subconscious mind exercise: Using the subconscious mind to enact a past, current or future events with your eyes closed.

Talking therapies: When only speech is used between therapist and client.

Template resources: Basic abilities and ingenuity a person can use for psychological guidance and direction.

Thought energy: The source of one's thinking.

Unconditional love: Instinctively giving love freely in any circumstances.

Validate: To confirm, prove true or accurate.

Visualisation: Forming pictures and feelings in the mind with the eyes closed.

Well-being: A state of being healthy, contented and at peace.

LAST WORDS

In writing this book 'Achieve What You Want in Life' I have used the experience of many years as a manager in the very competitive and tough commercial world, and then more than twenty years as a therapist helping people achieve what they want in life.

I would like you to enjoy a healthy, successful and fulfilled life. It is difficult to do this if your emotions and behaviour are frequently sabotaging all the hard work and effort you make to achieve the success in life you desire.

It isn't normally a problem for people to acquire practical skills and abilities in the job they have chosen to do and the life they want to lead, but are often held back from realising their full potential because their negative emotions and behaviour hold them back.

The aim of this book is to help the reader manage their mind and their life more effectively. I hope you have enjoyed the journey and you continue using the book to help you **enrich your life in a positive way.**

If you would like to contact Michael Dillon about any aspect of the book you can do so by writing to the publisher's email address:

info@newgeneration-publishing.com

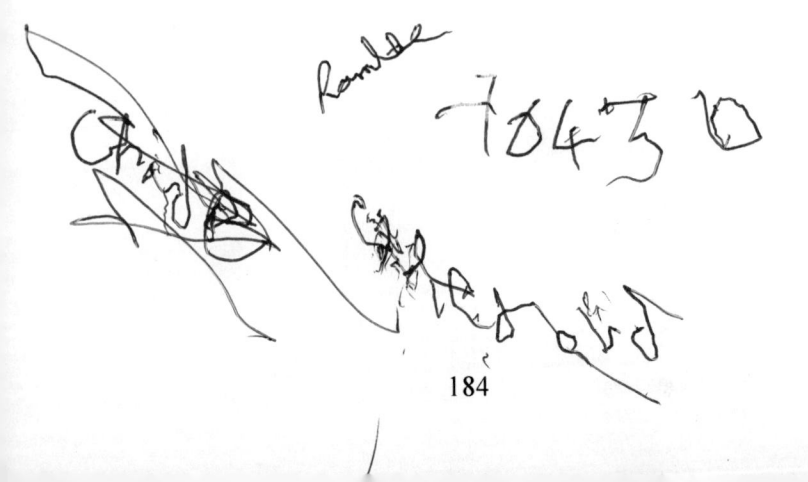